Housekeeping For The Soul

A Practical Guide to Restoring
Your Inner Sanctuary

First published by O-Books, 2010
O Books is an imprint of John Hunt Publishing Ltd., The Bothy, Deershot Lodge, Park Lane, Ropley,
Hants, SO24 0BE, UK
office1@o-books.net
www.o-books.net

Distribution in:	South Africa
	Stephan Phillips (pty) Ltd
UK and Europe	Email: orders@stephanphillips.com
Orca Book Services Ltd	Tel: 27 21 4489839 Telefax: 27 21 4479879
Home trade orders	
tradeorders@orcabookservices.co.uk	Text copyright Sandra Carrington-Smith 2008
Tel: 01235 465521	
Fax: 01235 465555	ISBN: 978 1 84694 281 5
Export orders	
exportorders@orcabookservices.co.uk	
Tel: 01235 465516 or 01235 465517	
Fax: 01235 465555	
USA and Canada	Design: Stuart Davies
NBN	
custserv@nbnbooks.com	All rights reserved. Except for brief quotations
Tel: 1 800 462 6420 Fax: 1 800 338 4550	in critical articles or reviews, no part of this
	book may be reproduced in any manner without
Australia and New Zealand	prior written permission from the publishers.
Brumby Books	
sales@brumbybooks.com.au	The rights of Sandra Carrington-Smith as author
Tel: 61 3 9761 5535 Fax: 61 3 9761 7095	have been asserted in accordance with the
	Copyright, Designs and Patents Act 1988.
Far East (offices in Singapore, Thailand,	
Hong Kong, Taiwan)	A CIP catalogue record for this book is available
Pansing Distribution Pte Ltd	from the British Library.
kemal@pansing.com	
Tel: 65 6319 9939 Fax: 65 6462 5761	Printed by Digital Book Print

O Books operates a distinctive and ethical publishing philosophy in
all areas of its business, from its global network of authors to
production and worldwide distribution.

Housekeeping For The Soul

A Practical Guide to Restoring
Your Inner Sanctuary

Sandra Carrington-Smith

BOOKS

Winchester, UK
Washington, USA

CONTENTS

Acknowledgements

It isn't every day that an author's dream of being published becomes reality, but it is indeed a rarity for that author to walk the path to publication alone. As someone told me just a few days ago, nobody in a team is less important than the next person. In a football team, although the star quarterback receives most attention, he is no more important than the "water boy." If you think he is, wait until you get thirsty; you might change your mind.

When I first embarked on my own amazing journey, I had sugar-plum dreams of writing a book and getting it published overnight. I envisioned agents and publishers fighting to represent and publish my work, and I assumed my mailbox would be filled with letters in no time at all. Then reality caught up with me. Rejection letters began to fill my mailbox instead, and the original manuscript was dissected several times before it even resembled anything a publisher might consider.

I spent so many hours working on the content and layout that I thought for sure my family was going to oust me, but they never did; instead, they supported the conception, pregnancy and delivery of my dream with a burst of patience and faith that was inspiring and profoundly touching.

Because of that, I would like to dedicate this book to my children, Stephen, Michael and Morgan, who enlightened my days with their bubbly personalities, and to my husband, John Carrington-Smith, who has always supported me in all my endeavors, one dream at a time. Many thanks to my parents, Diego and Cosetta Faiazza, my sister Patrizia, Bob and Ann Carrington-Smith and the rest of the Carrington-Smith clan, for their undying support.

I would like to thank my agent, Krista Goering, for believing in me when no one else would, and my publisher, John Hunt, for the timely work he puts in every day.

Of course, I can't forget all the friends who helped me with critique and proofreading: Dara Lyon-Warner, Pam Scarboro, and Natalie Kimber – each of you was a vital piece of this wonderful puzzle.

Finally, since most beautiful stories rightfully rely on a powerful ending, I would like to thank Dena Patrick, my editor. Dena, what can I say? Words cannot accurately describe your role in making my dream come true. I would like to say you are my right arm, but I can honestly admit that you are both my arms, eyes, ears and mouth. Your words of encouragement, your mind-blowing skills – both in marketing and editing – and your gentle yet explosive energy have propelled *Housekeeping for the Soul* to a level I never thought it could reach. For this I thank you from the bottom of my heart – I wouldn't have made it without you. Deep down, I know this is merely the beginning of a lifelong partnership and the first of many, many books.

Foreword

Imagine standing in front of an old house. At one time this structure was well-kept and inviting, but all you see are remnants of a home now in a complete state of disrepair. The flower beds are barren and desolate, with only shriveled remains of weeds. The exterior paint is faded, the chimney crumbling, and missing shingles expose the roof. As you carefully make your way along the cracked sidewalk to the front door you notice the windows are boarded up, blocking your view of the inside.

The door is unusually heavy, but you push it open and enter, only to find more damage.

Imagine now that the forbidding house is actually your life, the everyday reality you have erroneously created, inherited, or simply allowed for yourself.

Seeing the stark truth of the lives we inhabit can be a shock. For many it can be depressing, even frightening.

Once awakened to our situation, do we move forward with determination to change it or, faced with an overwhelming renovation, do we accept life as is, feeling we have no choice?

Just as a neglected, weathered house can be restored to its original beauty, the house of our soul can be revitalized and transformed into a nurturing abode where a wonderful life can flourish.

Within these pages is offered a new approach to emotional healing: Walking you through the house of your soul, room by room, using the familiar analogy of housecleaning.

My intention is to quite simply provide a strategy to improve your daily life, whether you are only in need of light dusting or whether a complete renovation is in order.

I also hope to empower each and every one of you by offering a new way to perceive your life situation. Nothing is ever completely hopeless. No matter how dismal our individual situation appears through the blindfold of illusion, there is always at least one path to follow that will lead us out of the darkness.

Please keep in mind that the first few chapters may be challenging to work through, but it's important for us to understand how we got here. Many of us are cleansing and organizing our inner selves for the very first time. Just as the initial efforts of renovating and cleaning a home—be it a house, apartment or other setting—are the most daunting, cleansing our inner world presents the same initial challenges. Once these first steps are behind us, the more enjoyable aspects of recreating ourselves can begin.

In the pages ahead we will explore the hidden reasons behind the gradual erosion of our lives. Each step of the way, I will provide tools to bring the house of your soul back to its original splendor, as well as tools to maintain your new reality.

We will approach this together, task by task, creating an internal space you will be grateful to inhabit and proudly share with others, a true reflection of your authentic self. Perhaps for the first time, you will be honored to call it "home".

Throughout this book I encourage you to explore the unknown which, for many, can seem so frightening. I gently guide you to explore the quiet caverns of your soul, just as you would the recesses of seldom-used closets or a forgotten attic. In doing so, you will expand your thoughts and perceptions, opening to new possibilities and ways of creating a new space within you and around you.

At the end of each chapter you will find simple affirmations, as well as a section entitled "A Taste of the Spiritual Unknown," where I share the ageless wisdom of various spiritual traditions for your reading pleasure and as another means of seeing life from a different vantage point.

After all, whether renovating or cleaning one's physical home, or cleansing and healing the house of our soul, it is good to take

2

a step back, look at the big picture, and try to see it from different perspectives. Only then you will truly be ready for the task of creating anew, in a manner that is in complete alignment with the most authentic you.

Sandra Carrington-Smith

www.sandracarringtonsmith.com

How I wish I could get inside my brain, to clean and organize it as easily as I do my house. First I'd take out the trash—all those negative thoughts that get in the way and keep me from doing my best work.
I'd bag up all those old hand-me-down ideas that clutter up my brain and don't fit me anymore. I'd suck up the cobwebs of less important thoughts so I could see my important ideas more clearly. I'd scrub the floor of complacency, allowing my passions to shine through. I'd wash the windows into my heart and soul so they could speak to me more openly. I'd analyze what I wanted to say and organize it into neat bundles. And finally, I'd decorate with pictures of good times, encouraging words, and smiles.

Elaine Luddy Klonicki

Chapter 1

Unlocking the Front Door
Fear of Change, Fear of the Unknown

Look not mournfully into the past. It comes not back again. Wisely improve the present. It is thine. Go forth to meet the shadowy future, without fear.
Henry Wadsworth Longfellow

As we stand in the open doorway, we finally see our home for what it is.

The thick protective walls and boarded windows had shielded us from looking outward at our environment. As for the interior, we had become so accustomed to our surroundings that we no longer noticed the disintegration. It was an insidious process, but we eventually became oblivious to the house of our soul.

But now we see—*really* see—and this new vision leads to awareness. As with anything, being aware is the first step.

Of course, at any crossroads in our lives we are given the opportunity to make a choice, to choose a path.

Who would choose to be unhappy or live in dismal conditions if they had the tools to change them? Why do we hesitate, delaying our shift to a better life?

The answer is simple: We are afraid of change. It's human nature. The fear of change—the fear of the unknown—is so great that we continue to live within the constraints of our own invisible walls.

Even with the resources to renovate, we fear our fragile structures will collapse and the foundation will crumble beneath us.

5

Fear isn't the only reason we resist change.

Force of habit is a considerable influence in our culture; habit is synonymous with stability while change is disconcerting. It stirs unrest, like a storm stirs the sediment in the sea; until the waters calm down and the sediment settles back to the bottom, the water appears cloudy.

We are very much creatures of habit. We eat, work and sleep at specific times, and have squeezed in multiple other activities, with little to no room for change.

In the midst of this structured life, most of us inevitably arrive at a point where change is necessary for survival. Because we never learned to easily accept change, we panic when we feel forced to make important decisions. Instead of embracing change as a new opportunity filled with adventure, we become almost paralyzed with fear.

Fear of change and force of habit can lead to another potentially harmful attitude: apathy. From an early age, we are taught to accept misery and limitation as a natural part of life.

As children we daydream of being knights and princesses, singers and ballerinas, but soon society tells us to grow up, accept the path in front of us and don't veer far from it. If a situation is uncomfortable, we are told to toughen up and bear with it. "It's life, get used to it."

We become desensitized and gradually forget our dreams. We stop giving attention to the things that make our hearts smile. We distract ourselves—and allow others to distract us—with no time in our day to think of such frivolous things as wishes, hopes and dreams. We must run, run, run, and be productive.

Unless we learn to create a bridge of balance between our dreams and the need to be responsible, we invite misery in.

No matter the circumstance of the invitation, misery is a willing companion. It creeps up on us silently and spreads to every part of our lives, invasive and aggressive as a virus. Misery becomes our identity, and we cling to it to justify our perceived failures.

Controlled by fear, we dig in and stay put, even if the walls are closing in. Renovation is too big a task. Many people have a hard enough time maintaining their lives on a day-to-day basis, and at times sheer survival takes hold and causes us to dig even deeper. We stay in miserable life situations, feeling we don't have the strength to change anything, until something pushes us to our limit and we must make a choice.

Make a choice. Choose your focus. That's how everything starts.

As scary as change can be, it doesn't have to be undertaken all at once. Sometimes small steps in the right direction are more beneficial than an explosive life-altering effort. Taking small steps, one day at a time, is less traumatic than rebuilding our entire identity from scratch.

Many times our fears aren't readily apparent. Sometimes we know what we want and pursue it with confidence, with no doubts. Or so we think. No matter how sure we are in our minds about a goal or desire, fears often lurk beneath the surface. In a later chapter we will explore the roles of our conscious and subconscious minds. When they work together, the possibilities are endless; when they are at odds, a mixed message is sent to the Universe.

For example, many mothers wish for a new job, something more exciting, more prestigious, and with better pay than their current job (including stay-at-home moms). However, such a job often comes with sacrifice. While not consciously worrying about the potential changes in their family's lives, there is a nagging sensation at the back of their minds on a subconscious level. They worry their families won't be cared for properly and that they will be failing their loved ones. This subconscious fear triggers blocks which manifest in the form of real-life obstacles for the individual.

This is self-sabotage, and we aren't even aware of it.

Another interesting form of self-sabotage is the marked aversion to living in the moment. We cling to the past, reliving old memories and repeatedly triggering emotions related to these flashbacks; or, we focus our full attention on the future. Rarely do we give attention to our Now.

I've often been asked, "But what if my Now is miserable? I don't want to feel that." This is a perfectly reasonable question. Ironically, I have also encountered those who gladly accept their current state of misery, as they firmly believe we all must suffer in order to be worthy of anything joyful, in this life and the next. We will explore both attitudes a little later and see how they act as blocks in the creation of a more fulfilling life.

For now, in this very moment as you are reading, I ask you to take a hard look at your present reality and accept where you are. Focus on your Now. If we were to die tomorrow, wouldn't it be best to make the most of what we have today rather than be concerned with yesterday or what may happen in the future?

If we focus on the moment, we are more likely to see the people we want to reach out to, and vice versa, as this moment is the only one that truly matters.

In the wonderful tales of Don Juan Matus, by Carlos Castaneda, we learn of the Toltec Indians' initiation of death, carefully designed to help facilitate understanding of this very important concept. In *Journey to Ixtlan*, Castaneda writes of the Angel of Death as a catalyst for embracing the Now. The Angel is near our left shoulder at all times; if we were to turn suddenly, we would likely catch a glimpse of this presence and realize Death is always near. With this in mind, we are more apt to savor each moment of our lives.

Everything in the Universe moves in perfect accord and constantly changes. Humans struggle with this concept, as we are not able to be fully in the moment until faced with extreme drama. When life is calm, the prospect of change triggers our old insecurities and we fight the current. We maintain our stronghold and desperately cling to the illusion of being in control of the events that affect our lives. We claim to want change but fear it at the same time. When in crisis, however, pure instinct kicks in.

A few years ago, my attention was piqued after hearing the story of a young woman who survived the tragic tsunami in Indonesia. During a brief interview the young woman explained that when she felt the water rushing past her, she knew she had to let go—both literally and figuratively—of any resistance, and allow the current to take her. She knew beyond any doubt that her willingness to let go and be led by the current brought her to safety.

If we can learn to tap into our innate wisdom and intuition, we will gradually become able to discern the difference between our fears based on insecurities versus our soul trying to steer us into the flow of least resistance. Change, and the strength to surrender to it, are an important part of our lives and should be viewed as an opportunity to experience wonderful things yet unseen.

When I first met my husband, John, I was still a teenager.

It was very exciting to meet someone from a different country and culture, and when the opportunity presented itself for me to move to the United States to be with him, I was ecstatic! My family could not understand why I was willing to undertake such a life-changing event. Having lived through the aftermath of World War II, my parents were all too familiar with the scenario of young girls meeting American soldiers and moving away. They heard many stories of love-struck girls finding themselves thrown into precarious situations, unhappy and unable to get back home.

My parents were a good example of clinging to the past and fearing change. Their fear as protective parents was certainly understandable; however, rather than see how genuinely happy I was, the images triggered in their minds were of poverty, hardship and loss of their daughter, all based upon what they had witnessed in the past.

In spite of their concern and disapproval, I chose to go forward with my plans. In November 1988, I made the big move and followed my first love (I was only seventeen when I met my husband and had just turned nineteen when I moved). I allowed myself to flow with the current.

On the day of my departure, I hopped on the plane destined to whisk me away from my home and country, with no fear in my heart. I did have a few doubts in the days before the departure, but I shut them down quickly; I wanted only love in my heart, not fear. I welcomed my new life with eagerness and hope. Within six months, John and I were married.

I realize I was very fortunate to have found such a good partner, and am grateful I chose to embrace him and our life together. I could have developed cold feet and never left Italy, or my situation could have been like one of those poor girls of the post-war era, but in the end it never was. John and I remain married, and the love I followed twenty years ago is still alive. Although we have endured many challenges and obstacles, our lives are happy and complete.

Some may say the courage and sense of adventure was attributable to my youth. The truth is I have continued to face life with only love in my heart, no fear, grateful for each experience and encounter along the way.

Each of us shall go through many changes in life, some wonderful and some less pleasant, but every experience has a purpose. If you can view life from that lens and be open to the lessons and opportunities for growth, you present yourself and those around you with a beautiful gift. We tell our children they learn through their mistakes, yet we often fail to recognize that, even in adulthood, life is a continual learning process.

The most amazing transformation I have witnessed in my

lifetime is that of a very close friend. Elizabeth always had a hard life: an overbearing father, extreme financial hardship as a child and adult, and a string of failed relationships. The house of the soul into which she was born and grew up was not one of nurturance and comfort.

Elizabeth could never find the door to get out of the depressing house; its walls trapped her and she felt imprisoned. She completely identified with hardship and introduced herself to the world with that calling card.

Her defensive and angry attitude eventually isolated her from friends and proved to be a solid barrier when she made attempts to date again, after her fifth marriage had failed.

The initial conversations with dates revolved around the wrongdoings and failings of former husbands; needless to say, the first dates were also the last. Elizabeth couldn't understand why no one called and why friends stayed away; she couldn't see that her behavior was a subconscious mechanism of self-defense, and that the perceived rejections from others only confirmed, in her mind, that she was not good enough.

She found herself completely alone, stuck in a miserable job and overwhelmed with debt. While she maintained a strong, defiant front, inside she was terrified. Through her fog of misery she couldn't imagine life getting any worse.

One morning I returned from running errands and found her sitting on my porch. Puzzled, I asked why she wasn't at the office, and she told me she had been fired.

I ran to her side to give her a hug. However, for the first time after such a big blow, she looked directly into my eyes and said, "It's going to be all right."

I froze. I would have bet against ever hearing her say those words; as it turned out, I would have happily lost my bet.

She said she was too tired to continue carrying the burdens of her life and didn't know where to turn or what to do, but she was also "tired of being tired".

This, combined with her spiritual beliefs, was the catalyst which initiated her shift. It didn't happen overnight, but it did happen.

As of that day, Elizabeth's life took a noticeable turn. She made a conscious decision to change her inner landscape. The tears began to dry and she smiled more often. Even when it seemed she was entering a dark tunnel, something positive would happen at the last minute.

Finally, her years of spiritual exploration fell into place like pieces of a puzzle. Applying the concepts to her life for the first time, she simply made a choice and shifted how she saw herself and how she presented herself to the world, trusting that everything would be okay.

Today, Elizabeth is at peace. She is moving forward in all aspects of her life, including financial stability, and has learned to accept herself for who she is and what she has to offer. She no longer sees her identity as the one she grew up with. She acts much differently around her friends now and has attracted more people into her circle.

As with the girl caught in the tsunami, Elizabeth recognized change was needed. She relinquished control and allowed the current to transport her safely to the other side, trusting that she would be fine. And she is.

What is a bit harder for people to come to terms with is that, even after they make the decision to change, they may still have to go through the residue of their past choices and the energetic imprints of their previous attitudes.

Many masters and spiritualists have told us that all we have to do is visualize our goals and they will come true.

It is my firm belief and experience that, in one form or another, our thoughts do indeed manifest in our reality. It is also my belief that what we are living today is the manifestation of yesterday's thoughts. The new, changed thoughts we formulate today will be the reality of tomorrow.

With the release of *The Secret* and the concept of our thoughts creating reality being more widely accepted, many have diligently worked to abide by these spiritual principles. They have maintained positive thoughts with pure intentions for extended periods of time, only to be slapped in the face by more misfortune. This newfound positive approach to life, still as shaky as a baby taking his first steps, is so fragile that one single blow can be shattering, pulling them back into the black hole of negative thinking.

There is a good reason for the saying "patience is a virtue", and why faith is paramount in changing one's life.

Faith in oneself is indeed at the base of any transformation. When a situation appears dire, we must hold on to the certainty that things will change. Rather than dive deeper into the abyss of despair, know that your current drama will shift.

Mother Nature offers many perfect mirrors of this *knowingness* as a concept of survival. Regardless of how dark the night, the sun always rises the following morning.

She also displays the need to go through periodic trials in order to remain strong. Thunderstorms roll through felling trees, yet in reality they eradicate the old and weak, creating more fertile conditions for the new to thrive. The trees that do survive damaging winds develop stronger roots and brave each subsequent storm with more ease. Within nature, there are harsh cleansings which are necessary for the survival of many species, yet the cycles of growth and renewal continue.

Similarly, each time we are caught in a life storm, we are easily swept into the whirlwinds of fear and doubt, and forget about the cyclical nature of all things. We survive the birth and death of loved ones, health crises, marital challenges, and financial uncertainties. While we stand in the midst of the storm it feels as though it will never pass, but most dramas do run out of steam and come to an end. If we could see life storms for what they truly are, we would see they are vital to our continued well-being by creating fertile ground for inner growth.

No matter how harsh the storms of destiny may be, their task is not to destroy us; they offer the opportunity to remove our weaknesses, helping us to heal and grow stronger. If we can try to understand their role and be thankful, the storms will pass and the sun will soon be shining again.

It is also important to realize when professional assistance might be needed. Please be honest with yourself and consider whether there is any possibility the emotional pain or distress in your life can be attributed to a medical condition. Please also consider that if the storms in your life have been severe, perhaps counseling or support groups are an appropriate path for you.

Even though severe storms can leave our physical homes in need of expert care, the damage is reparable; so, too, is any damage to the house of our soul.

We all know people who seem to handle stormy weather— challenges much more severe than our own—with grace and ease. It is a lesson in humility to note how others *react* to life's harsh blows. While not everything in life is within our complete control, our reactions are, as are our choices.

We can choose to accept any perceived setbacks as storms testing our courage, offering an opportunity for growth, or as an unkind destiny with the intent to destroy our spirit. Let's choose to move forward with hope. After all, if the negative thoughts can become reality, it stands to reason that our new positive attitude will eventually manifest in a positive reality as well.

Are you ready to accept the job of recreating your life? Together we shall create your own "Extreme Makeover: House of the Soul Edition".

Chapter 1: Affirmations
I open the door to my inner self, I welcome change

- I see the house of my soul, and observe for the first time all the damage I refused to acknowledge before.
- I know that this awareness is my first step toward healing, so I look at the door with increasing courage.
- I feel the fear of change melting away, as my resolve to heal my reality grows and becomes stronger with each step on the path to meeting my inner self.
- I peer through the windows and catch a glimpse of my true self: a timeless, ageless, genderless and perfect expression of the mind of creation.

Chapter 1: A Taste of the Spiritual Unknown
One of my favorite sayings is, "A shift in perspective can drastically alter your perception of reality". It is my personal mission to offer people ways to see the world differently.

Having grown up in Italy in a very unconventional home in which two seemingly different spiritual practices were faithfully followed (Catholicism and Voodoo—yes, Voodoo), I grew to understand that, at the core, the two religions are very similar. The outside perception is that they are very different—even at odds with one another—but from decades of experience I see it from a completely different point of view. This early lesson in perceptions has enabled me to create a full, diverse, loving life experience.

In *Housekeeping for the Soul*, I attempt to share these lessons in order to encourage greater awareness and a more expansive way of thinking.

Within each of these sections entitled "A Taste of the Spiritual Unknown", I offer enlightening bits of information, with examples of spiritual traditions and rituals as they pertain to the chapter's subject matter. I will often refer to Voodoo and other mysterious ancient belief systems to show how similar all paths are at their foundation.

It is most certainly not my intention to convert anyone or to encourage anyone to follow a particular path. I respect all paths, as well as those who follow no particular path. I simply share a little of my knowledge of this mostly unknown, misunderstood path of Voodoo as a way to stretch the mind and shift perceptions.

Although most of the world's spiritual traditions focus on healing and ascension by following different paths, Voodoo is probably the most colorful and participatory, and offers a taste of true spirituality carefully hidden within the worship of the charming Orishas. Orishas are Spirit's helpers, elevated expressions of the Creator, known to have been humans before their celestial promotion. The Orishas are very much like the Catholic saints and correspond to one another; indeed, the history of Catholicism and Voodoo are deeply entwined.

Before going further, it will perhaps be helpful to give you even more insight into my spiritual background. I have already mentioned Voodoo and Catholicism being part of my upbringing. In addition, my maternal grandmother was a Strega witch, a devotee of a tradition centered on a centuries-old practice of Italian witchcraft, and my paternal grandmother a Christian healer.

I am certainly a fusion of all of these practices, yet I mostly resonate with the path of Voodoo. I believe that the vision of healing is the same in most traditions, and I can only share information from the tradition I know best to bring clarity to the fact that beauty and healing are found within all practices, even those that have been corrupted and demonized through lack of knowledge and fear of the unknown.

Voodoo is believed to be the world's oldest religion, having originated in West Africa. Western religions and modern media have painted an evil and unfair portrait of Voodoo, often visualized as an evil magician sticking pins in a doll with the express intent of causing harm. Nothing is further from the truth.

The practical, hands-on aspect of the religion is expressed through what has come to be known as "hoodoo" which, among other things, is the working of spells (known as "roots") with the intent of helping others overcome their obstacles through the invocation of divine intervention. In my experience, the vast majority of Voodoo practitioners are kind-hearted individuals who use their skills and gifts to help others. As in all religions and spiritual practices, there are no doubt charlatans. This is why we must learn to tap into our intuition when seeking guidance from others and when learning about various paths of healing. With that said, it is time for authentic practitioners of these ancient religions to reclaim the inherent goodness of what they offer.

One interesting element of Voodoo is that all Orishas are represented as dual entities. It is common belief among the Yoruban people (where it is believed Voodoo originated, often spelled Vodou or Voudou) that every person and object has a twin, serving as its opposite.

Within the colorful pantheon of the Voodoo Orishas, one entity is revered above all and must be called upon first, to open the doorway to Spirit and before other Orishas may be called. The name varies by regional tradition but is collectively known as Eshu-Elegba, reflecting the paradox of duality embraced by the Yorubans. He is known as both a divine spirit and the devil, and thus symbolizes the crossroads. If properly respected and revered, Elegba is said to aid humans in opening doors to their hidden fears so that they can be carried to the surface, face them, and release them.

The following is a popular hoodoo root, often used to ask Elegba to help us overcome a crossroads in our life with which we are struggling.

On a Monday, preferably at dawn, the practitioner will go to a four-way crossroads and bring Elegba a small offering of liquor, a cigar, three coins, and a small piece of paper on which is written in lead pencil what is being asked of him. After making the request, the practitioner will leave the area and go back home, following a different path than the one used to get there.

The association of the physical crossroads to the emotional crossroads helps the practitioner in letting go of the overwhelming weight of his fears and worries. By making use of tangible symbols in this ritual, the person is able to more easily release the negative energy associated with their particular problem and focus on the positive aspects of their life.

Welcome to your first taste of the Spiritual Unknown.

Chapter 2

Clearing a Path Through the Clutter
Create Space, Create Time

One of the advantages of being disorderly is that one is constantly making exciting discoveries.
A.A. Milne

Everyone is familiar with the image of a cluttered home. It can feel like the walls are closing in and there's not enough room to take a deep breath.

That's exactly how I feel after my husband and three children have been home all weekend. My home is usually fairly tidy, but after the weekend it looks like a tornado came through!

Each Monday morning I take my cup of coffee and reluctantly begin to inspect the damage. Everything seems out of place, with little fingerprints everywhere and toys having migrated to the most unthinkable places. There isn't one area free of clutter. My first instinct is the same, week after week: *Grab your car keys and get out as fast as you can!*

The amount of work ahead appears insurmountable as I stand in the midst of it all, looking for excuses to avoid the dreadful task. Then I remind myself what I need to do to get started.

As soon as my children leave for school, the first thing I do is clear the kitchen table. This is where I sit back and regroup, assessing the amount of work each room requires. I need this open, uncluttered space before I can tackle the project and restore order to the rest of my home.

The same applies when we are trying to cleanse and restore order to our lives.

In Chapter One we acknowledged something must change in our lives and have made the decision to do just that. We're ready to dive in, we're motivated to start our inner spring cleaning, but where do we begin?

An overwhelmed mind runs in circles around the problem at hand rather than tackling what needs to be done. There is no focus. In order to formulate a plan, with a starting point, we need to have a clear space where we can gather our thoughts.

We also need quiet time so that we can free up energy for the tasks at hand. How this is done varies with each individual; some people need physical space to call their own in order to think clearly, while others only need a few minutes of meditation or "time to breathe" to be refreshed and make sound decisions.

Being still and quiet so that we can listen to our inner guidance has become a quaint idea. The bulk of our days are spent in some level of frenzy, attending to myriad errands and responsibilities, feeling guilty if we can't fit it all in.

Parents are familiar with the long hours spent in the car, driving from one activity to the next, smothered by never-ending demands. Today's "good parents" are supposed to run themselves ragged, working their lives around the hectic schedules created for their children.

Because we have not allowed our children any quiet time, they won't know how to be alone or entertain themselves without the companionship of their iPods, cell phones, and videos. We are not setting a very good example, in my opinion, and our children are being conditioned to constantly require external stimuli.

Those who don't have children are expected to be equally as busy, running between work and social obligations. Everyone stays so busy. Sadly, those blessed or wise enough to not lead a hectic life are often made to feel guilty, as though they are not working hard enough or doing their best.

As we wade through the river of demands and expectations, we often forget ourselves. We lose sight of who we are. If you had to describe yourself, could you? Could you step back and see yourself objectively?

We rarely take time to assess what is really going on in our lives. There is certainly no time for nurturing the spirit or listening to inner guidance. It's one thing to go with the flow of life; it's another to not even realize there is a flow.

It is rare to find an individual who is comfortable sitting in silence, allowing his or her mind to be still. Perhaps this is intentional, more than we care to admit.

My husband is a prime example of this concept. His work is very demanding and the days blur from one to another as he interacts with customers and personnel, often listening to complaints from both throughout his day.

As if he didn't have enough noise and stimuli in his day, as soon as he leaves work he jumps in his car and blasts the radio; once he gets home, the television becomes the main focus of his attention until he falls asleep. Nevertheless, he frequently complains of stress from the lack of personal, quiet time.

In actuality he could have a decent amount of personal time. After the children go to bed, he has several hours to call his own. Once a week he shoots pool with relatives and friends and, when weather and work permit, he plays golf and goes fishing.

From the outside looking in he appears to have extra time, so why does he constantly feel stressed, even when away from work?

It's a choice. The time he could easily claim as quiet time is filled with social activity and nonstop outside stimuli. He chooses to fill his time, replacing one source of preoccupation with another.

It is my belief that he is like so many who, for whatever reason, resist being alone...and resist being in silence.

We all know people who seem afraid to be alone. They always need to be with someone, on the phone, or online interacting in some way.

We are all at risk of doing this in one way or another. There are many more distractions in our modern world: 24-hour television with hundreds of stations, the Internet, iPods, Blackberries...all with the potential to distract, preventing us from having a chat with ourselves.

In Chapter One we briefly met Elizabeth, a close friend who was able to create change in her life by making a deliberate choice.

Elizabeth did not like to be alone; as long as she was surrounded by people, she could escape facing the deeply insecure parts of herself that she wasn't ready to accept. Whereas some people with similar emotional blocks try to shun others and stay isolated, Elizabeth needed constant interaction; this was her distraction from herself.

As with most people mired in negativity, Elizabeth had a myopic, limited perception. She interpreted every interaction as deeply personal. When her old self-perception was holding her hostage, she expected people to abandon her, to treat her unfairly, and to demean her because, deep down, she was doing that to herself. She repeatedly attracted people into her life who would confirm this image, people who would treat her with the same value scale that she used to measure herself. Of course, these were all subconscious triggers; she was never overtly aware of this pattern.

All she knew was that she longed for companionship, yet the people in her life were ignoring her for reasons she did not understand. I recall one particular incident when Elizabeth's misperceptions led to a conflict between us.

I had a newborn, two older children, a husband, and an assortment of daily chores. Time for myself, let alone time for friends, was literally nonexistent. I had only one friend I treasured when time availed itself: sleep.

Elizabeth called frequently to say hello, and I often had to let the answering machine pick up. If had a minute or two, I would call back, but many times I couldn't. It wasn't that I did not want to call her back; there were simply not enough minutes in my day. To her, the fact that I would not call back right away or that I sounded distracted when I finally did was a clear sign that I was about to abandon her.

Today Elizabeth has learned to put herself in the other person's shoes and not take everything personally. She now enjoys interactions with others without her thoughts filled with worry and doubt. Perhaps most importantly, she has grown to enjoy the pleasure of her own company and can be silent, alone with only her thoughts and dreams in a space she now treasures.

Let's imagine we finally have the opportunity to clear a little corner in our home to be our "quiet place," where we can think or read or daydream. As the day goes along, every time we clear one piece of clutter from our intended space, we replace it with another piece picked up elsewhere within the home or brought in from the outside.

At the end of the day, we have not achieved our goal of creating this special space. Instead, all we have done is replace clutter with clutter, and wasted our energy in the process. We stayed busy but ultimately invested our time and energy in creating an illusion.

As we try to connect with our true selves, we must understand this concept and be vigilant to avoid this pattern. We need to be brutally honest and recognize that we fill our lives with clutter—sometimes intentionally, sometimes passively—but we allow it just the same. Anything to avoid being alone with ourselves.

Most are running from something...a memory, a feeling, an abandoned dream. It is very hard to know what we are running away from until we've taken time to listen, but the whispers we hear from within can be distressing. It's easier to contain our thoughts and emotions rather than face them. However, by doing this, we only increase the pressure within.

Picture a pot of water on the stove, lid intact, burner on low. Now imagine we are the pot, and our thoughts and emotions are the water. On a daily basis we encounter a variety of situations, each one triggering an emotional response within us. Most often we don't discuss it or give it much attention; we just bite our tongues and keep going. We let the pot of water simmer with the lid on, blocking the steam from escaping. Every day, we add to the pot, occasionally turning the heat up or down, but never releasing steam. We just turn up the radio or television so we don't hear the rattle of the lid or the steam hissing.

When it finally boils over we stare at the pot in surprise and then get agitated about the mess. Had we taken the time to remove the lid and release steam, the water would not have boiled over.

Once again we perpetuate our state of discontent, resisting the natural flow until we are forced by a crisis.

Relieving this inner pressure does not require a lot of time. Ten minutes a day is often enough to clear away the clutter in our minds. Sit still and observe the internal chatter, acknowledge it, take deep breaths and let it flow, without questioning or overanalyzing. Let it be, and it will gradually dissipate.

I will discuss the often misunderstood nature of meditation later but, for now, consider this: The term *meditation* is very similar to the word *mediation*. It's as though we are mediating our thoughts when trying to achieve a state of mental stillness.

You can also accomplish this stillness through a quiet walk, gardening, or any solitary activity where the only voice you hear is your own.

Reading is a form of meditation; it is a focused activity which enables us to shut out the rest of the world, absorbing the wisdom or sheer entertainment value of the written word. It is most beneficial when the words impart inspiring, healing messages, or when we allow ourselves to get lost in a good story, releasing daily worries.

Somehow we must remove the incessant needless distractions from our lives. We need time to go within and listen. More than anything we need to stop running from ourselves.

If we don't put forth effort to try to hear our own voice, why should we expect anyone else to listen to us?

Learning to do this can take time, but people have grown impatient, another symptom of our fast-paced lifestyle of instant gratification.

I'm frequently asked if there is a fast way to "go within" and overcome obstacles. The answer is yes and no.

Every true healing requires commitment and a fundamental restructuring of thought patterns; it is a long-term process. Short-term healing can be achieved by exploring and addressing the situations that trigger the most powerful reactions. By taking positive, proactive steps toward what is holding us back, we can certainly create a springboard to help us tackle the deeper blocks stored within the mind's recesses. One by one, we will take down the walls that both prevent us from looking outside and from going within.

Meanwhile, we must focus on creating and maintaining time and space for ourselves. It is within this space that we can slowly reconnect with the collective consciousness. The white noise infiltrating our lives not only removes us from our selves, it desensitizes us to everything and everyone. As we create this quiet, clear space to focus on becoming reacquainted with our heartfelt hopes and dreams, we can become more sensitive to the hopes and dreams of others.

Consider that, as you heal yourself, you are also working toward healing Humanity. If you believe as I do that we are all connected, then our individual wellness is necessary for the wellness of the Whole. Paying attention to your basic needs is the first step toward being of true service to others.

Changing the world does not always involve paramount actions; it starts with an act of random kindness, whether it is directed to the self or others. If we give water to a thirsty dog, we have already taken a step in changing that dog's world; if we offer a helping hand to a stranger, we have taken a step in changing their world; if we create a sacred space for ourselves, we take a step in changing our own world which creates ripples that will change the world of others.

Within this space there is room for our inner light to grow and join with the light of others. The dim light of one candle might be bright enough to expose the path to our front door, but the light of a thousand candles will make all paths visible and all obstacles illuminated.

Chapter 2: Affirmations

I am comfortable being in complete silence, alone with my thoughts and dreams

- As I listen to myself, I find peace in my world.
- The house of my soul can be restored.
- I create a neutral space from where I clearly observe what needs to be done.
- I must remember that I am worthy of being listened to; I put forth effort to listen to myself.

Chapter 2: A Taste of the Spiritual Unknown

Given the hectic nature of the modern world, it is nearly impossible to imagine the slow-paced life of thousands of years ago. Today we must sift through the maze of distractions to find peace and tranquility. In ancient times, however, life was much simpler. Even so, they were in search of comforting, reliable signs in their world to create a sense of stability and know they were not alone.

There were three reliable elements in their world: the sun, the moon and the stars.

The sun became the God, the moon the Goddess, and the stars the various embodiments through the constellations, which became the basis of the zodiac.

It's easy to see how deity status was bestowed upon the sun and the moon; the ancients learned that, without either, their world would cease to exist. The sun provided daylight and warmth and helped their crops grow. The moon's phases affected tides and, many still believe, plants and animal behavior, and became the basis of cycles and calendar systems.

Since ancient times, the new moon is seen as the birthing cycle of the moon's phases. Just as ancients saw this time as the best time to plant seeds for their crops, many today continue to perform rituals during which they sow the seeds of their desires and intentions. The darkness of the new moon offers a nurturing environment where these seeds take root and grow throughout the moon's cycle, hopefully coming to fruition by the time of the full moon.

Throughout time, the sun, moon and stars have helped humans make sense of their world. Whether leading stressful modern-day lives, or simpler lives of pure survival, we always seek clarity as we move through this life.

When Catholics are in need of clarity, they are taught to pray to St. Clare of Assisi, the Patroness of those with sore eyes. Having committed herself to a life of poverty, caring for those afflicted with disease—especially blindness—St. Clare is attributed with healing vibrations connected to sight. The name Clare means "shining" and "clear".

In the Voodoo tradition the corresponding Orisha to the energy of St. Clare is known as Klemezin.

As we humans are known to resist releasing our emotional attachments, and because they are often so powerful they have fused with our own energy, our ego manipulates our perception to cause us temporary blindness; if we don't see the patterns, then we won't be able to reach the hidden triggers. Klemezin is called upon to achieve the necessary clarity for healing.

When asking for Klemezin's help, we will need a bowl of water, mixed with a bit of coconut juice, shredded coconut and white flower petals. The bowl is presented to Klemezin and placed under the bed of the person who wishes to achieve clarity, after the sheets have been changed. The next morning, the water must be sprinkled around the room, with some of it used to wash the individual's eyes for healing clarity. Customarily, after requesting a miracle of clarity, financial offerings are taken to a charity institution which benefits children and the poor.

Chapter 3

The Big Picture
Perspectives and Perceptions – The
Diamond Theory

*When you look at it in a mean way, how mean it is! When you look at
it selfishly, how selfish it is! But when you look at it in a broad,
generous, friendly spirit, what wonderful people you find in it.*
Horace Rutledge

By this point, we have made our choice. We recognized the need
for change, created the space to go within, and now it is time to
come up with a plan of action.

This is where I encourage you to take a deep breath and try
look at the bigger picture before moving ahead. Make good use
of that sacred space carved out of the clutter to look at your
situation in a new light. View the house of your soul from
different angles, different vantage points. Let's start by remem-
bering that our external circumstances do not always reflect our
internal state of being.

Many individuals are living in grim conditions, including
homelessness, yet they close their eyes and see with their hearts
the potential in front of them. The house of their soul is a house
of plenty as they strive to find beauty and comfort in the smallest
of things. Others lead lives of opulence, ensconced in beautiful
estates, but their souls are in a state of poverty, never able to find
nourishment or experience joy.

We are the only ones who know the truth and can accurately
assess our own lives. Now that we *truly see*, it's time to put it all
into perspective.

Perception and perspective are ever-changing concepts that affect every area of our lives, creating the filter through which we form our beliefs.

Early in life our viewpoints are often the same as our parents; we listen to adult conversations and use that information to shape what we believe in our own minds. This is a passive process; as children we overhear conversations and, without realizing it, incorporate elements of these discussions into our psyche, our self-image, and our outlook on life. Children are like sponges; they easily absorb the opinions and beliefs of their caregivers, using these to form their own.

It's as though we go through our formative years thinking with someone else's mind. Many of us still hold onto our parents' opinions into adulthood; when we start forming our own opinions, it may feel as though we are betraying them.

The opinions and beliefs absorbed as children continue to impact us as adults in ways we never consider. Even casual things overheard as a child can seep into our subconscious and affect us intensely.

I recently discovered a hidden block within me which I could trace back to my earliest memories.

When I was very little I recall hearing bits and pieces related to my birth, and the consequent death of my twin. I heard adults saying, "She must have been the stronger one, that's why she survived." My mother would make comments such as, "Yes, the doctor thought I was gaining too much weight and put me on a diet. The other little girl probably starved because Sandra was the stronger one and took all the nourishment."

I never really thought about these conversations nor did I consider their impact. As a small child, they simply registered in my mind and simmered in my subconscious.

As years went by and my spiritual path pushed me to delve deeper within myself, I realized there were emotional triggers that I had not yet explored. One day, quite by accident, I was talking to a friend about the fact that I am a twin. As those forgotten memories rose to the surface, the emotional charge associated with the recollection was tremendous. I was overwhelmed with grief and sadness.

It wasn't until that very moment that the realization hit me full force: I had internalized a sense of guilt, as though I was responsible for the death of my twin sister. This subconscious trigger had been there my entire life and, in hindsight, clearly affected me in many ways.

By bringing it to the surface and examining it with my adult mind, I immediately understood there was no cause for guilt or any sense of responsibility on my part. My heart ached for the pain I must have felt as a child taking on such a huge, silent burden.

Once the block came to light, I acknowledged it, accepted how it had affected me, and then released it.

I recommend keeping an open mind about how such misperceptions and misinterpretations in childhood have affected us, especially when conflicts arise.

It is interesting to note how those growing up in the nineties have a distinctly different perspective from those raised in "pre-Internet" years.

Their view of life is not confined in any way. With the widespread availability of the Internet, a multitude of world views and opinions are suddenly there for all to absorb. The new generation's life perspectives are shaped by the world, beyond the boundaries of their family, their community, and their country of origin.

Children will always be influenced by those closest to them, but it is interesting to observe the more expansive outlook the younger generation embraces. The words "boundaries" and "limitations" are, in general, not part of their vocabulary.

How we perceive both our inner and outer worlds is greatly influenced by our vantage point. If we shift our position ever so slightly, it's possible to have a completely new perception of an idea or situation.

The power of perspective is a vital tool to employ as we work on the house of our soul.

Many cultures believe the perspective-perception concept is one of the most important life lessons. In African lore, for example, one of the most well-known entities is Eshu.

Eshu is a trickster god, a benevolent-yet-prankster spirit, who confuses people in order to impart knowledge and teach fundamental life lessons.

In one of the folk stories, Eshu walks down a dirt road between two rivaling farms. He wears a red and black hat; the hat is black on one side, red on the other. After he has passed the farms and can no longer be seen, the two farmers come together, asking questions about the stranger with the hat. The first farmer insists that he saw a stranger wearing a black hat, while the second farmer insists he saw the same stranger, with the same clothes, but he swears up and down that the hat was red.

As the two farmers continue arguing about the color of the hat, the stranger comes walking back up the road, this time in the opposite direction.

The farmers then realize they were both right; they saw what was in front of them and assumed the other person saw the exact same thing. They never considered the perspective from the other side.

As we try to understand the intangible world of perception, I will now introduce another good family friend.

Joe is an interesting and complex man; to this day, he is probably one of the saddest men I know. He has always lived lavishly but has never felt accomplished in anything.

During childhood Joe and his brother were viewed by their parents as Cain and Abel. When Joe showed that he was more rebellious and determined to have his way, his parents sent him off to boarding school. Once out of school, he was thrust into the family business to work side by side with his brother. In his desire to please his father, Joe never revealed that he hated the business and wanted no part of it.

Years went by and the two brothers approached their careers in different ways. Joe was conducting his business outside the office, making connections that would prove vital to the financial standing of the firm, while his brother put his heart into administration and management of the business. From a financial point of view, Joe was the spender while his brother was the penny-pincher.

A few years ago, newly divorced and alone, Joe fell into a deep depression and rarely left his apartment. Once he was able to pull his head above the murky, viscous waters of a mental breakdown, he returned to the office. However, he felt his presence was ignored by the employees and by his brother.

Joe took that personally and felt excluded from the very business he helped build.

The two brothers were like strangers. There were certainly other aggravating factors playing a role, but the core problem was that neither was willing to look at things from a different perspective. Both remained anchored in their own perception of the facts, compromising their relationship on a professional and personal basis.

So, who was at fault and who was right? Truthfully, as in the folktale of Eshu and the hat, both were right.

Joe was right in that he had indeed contributed substantially to the firm's success and was entitled to a role in decision-making within the business. He was also correct in feeling betrayed by his brother, who had not been completely honest about a stock transaction which took place during Joe's divorce crisis.

On the other hand, his brother was also right. He was the one at the office, day in and day out, dealing with clients and personnel. He also had the rightful claim to having saved every penny for the benefit of the company, while his brother went out and used business funds to finance his luxurious lifestyle.

It is obvious both brothers were right—and wrong—on some level. However, if they could walk in one another's shoes, they would understand the big picture much better. A truce could certainly be attained, but to this day both brothers choose to keep their walls intact, with no communication.

Now that the importance of perception has been discussed using several real-life examples, it is time to introduce the Diamond Theory.

Diamonds are one of nature's marvels. If properly cut by a master jeweler, these precious gems are extremely valuable and breathtakingly beautiful. Once a raw diamond is professionally cut, the light it emanates is spectacular.

Each facet reflects a different color of light, which changes when the diamond is moved or when the individual looks at it from different angles. The diamond itself does not change; what changes is the way we are looking at it. If we shift slightly, our perception of the light radiating from the facets will shift.

Let's imagine that we can physically merge with another person who is also staring at the same gem.

If it were physically possible to simultaneously stand in the *same exact spot* as the other person and look at the diamond with eyes on the *same exact* level, then we would see *exactly* the same facet of the diamond.

The Diamond Theory is as simple as this: Just as the light of the unmoving diamond remains the same, so do the details of a situation or life event; what changes is the perception of those who experience it.

Our perception will remain different from others if we insist on maintaining our rigid perspective while evaluating an object or situation. If we try to look at things from where the other person is standing, our perception will inevitably change.

It is wise to trust our own judgment but remain flexible enough to accept that there are other valid viewpoints. As Nietzsche said, "You have your way. I have my way. As for the right way, the correct way, and the only way, it does not exist."

As you step back and take in the big picture, be compassionate in your assessment; usually, the harshest and most twisted perception of all is the one we have of ourselves.

I have encountered individuals who appear on the surface to be very self-assured, and I have met others who seem to doubt their own shadow. Both self-images are probably the result of inherent personality traits and the influence of others, beginning in childhood. We will take a look at both self-image types to further this discussion.

To better understand the first type we will take a glimpse into the life of Angel.

The first impression of Angel is that of an outgoing man with a loving wife, two healthy children, and a successful career making use of his many skills and talents.

One quickly learns that Angel has had many different jobs over the years. As he tells it, when he is first hired it is as though he is God's gift to the company and can do no wrong. He regales his audience with tales of superiors being smitten by his talent and teamwork, and always brags about wonderful career advancements that are offered to him almost immediately.

I met him shortly after he received a promotion which involved extensive travel. He never missed the chance to tell of his great success and how his promotion to management led to the company flourishing beyond expectations.

According to Angel, his boss was amazed and was most certainly going to promote him to district manager.

The next thing we knew, Angel had been fired, suddenly and without warning. His explanation varied from conversation to conversation. In one he said this was due to company mergers and management changes; in another he said they couldn't afford him; in yet another he said he was let go because his talent threatened the executives.

I soon learned that this same pattern had manifested throughout his life. He is the Messiah for a short time and the pariah soon after.

The same was true for friendships, as people would tire of his megalomania and compulsion to be the center of attention. Eventually, things at home deteriorated as well.

In his eyes, however, Angel could do no wrong. So, where is the disconnect?

The problem is that Angel is only self-assured on the surface. As seen with Elizabeth before her transformation, Angel comes through very strong and paints an image that impresses people at first. Beneath the surface, he is deeply insecure.

If we look back at his childhood, like Elizabeth, Angel was told he could do nothing right. His father was loud and aggressive, and physically abused him. He grew up comparing himself to his successful sister, who was seen as perfect by his father. Angel always felt that he had to jump higher, achieve more, and speak louder to have any hope of winning attention for himself.

Underneath the false exterior, Angel is deeply insecure and views life as nonstop competition. His inner triggers constantly put him in a position where he ends up confirming his own inadequacy. He regularly loses everything and must start over because, at his core, he feels undeserving.

If Angel could come to accept that he has innate value and deserves to be happy and secure, his life would truly begin to shift.

As we continue to explore perception of the self, it is time to meet Gabriella.

Gabriella's parents are immigrants who moved to the United States from Mexico when she was a toddler, along with another child and few possessions.

From early childhood Gabriella had strong attachment to her mother, while the relationship with her father was marred by his favoritism toward the older sister.

While her sister was consistently praised for her successes, Gabriella was deprived of any attention. When labeled as having a learning disability, her self-image declined even further, as did the relationship with her father. He never missed a chance to belittle her in front of others, planting the seed in her mind that she had no value.

Her father's belligerent, demeaning attitude resulted in Gabriella learning very early on how to be invisible. She grew to hate being in crowds and detested social affairs. As an adult, Gabriella expected all men to be like her father: loud, threatening and verbally abusive. Indeed, a pattern quickly developed, with Gabriella only attracting men who were like her father. Within these relationships she withdrew from interaction and rarely ventured out of her shell to show how she honestly felt. She assumed no one was interested, as she had nothing of value to share. She had a very hard time accepting anything positive in her life, as she never felt she deserved any of them.

Although their childhoods were similar, Gabriella and Angel reacted differently to the verbal and mental abuse inflicted upon them. As adults, neither believes they deserve happiness or love, but they express their pain and feelings of inadequacy differently. Angel always struggles to place himself in the spotlight, while Gabriella makes herself disappear.

During the years dedicated to being a life coach, I have met many people similar to Angel and Gabriella. The common denominator among all of them was the internal void, though few could recall the source of their emptiness and pain. The vast majority had no hope that life could change; they were convinced the same patterns would repeat, over and over again. After a certain point, most *consciously* and overtly believed they were unworthy rather than it being merely a subconscious trigger.

It is likely we all know someone who resembles Angel or Gabriella. Their stories are not unique, but they show how pervasive this struggle is despite the plethora of resources available to improve one's self-esteem.

Stepping back and learning to see patterns from different perspectives, and realizing how the words and actions of others have shaped our thoughts and self-image is one of the first items on our to-do list.

We must also see that nothing is irreparable. We can rebuild and recreate ourselves to be a truer reflection of our soul.

There is no discussion of blame here. In most cases of abuse, be it emotional or physical, the perpetrator was also abused at some point. So many people are victims of victims. However, as adults we must accept responsibility for our choices and actions and not deflect the need to be accountable for our own life path.

With the resurgence of teachings concerning the association between mind and soul, a new place of prominence has been given to the word "forgiveness". Many of us on a spiritual path have been conditioned to believe that by forgiving a painful action we are forfeiting our right to receive human or cosmic justice, but nothing is further from the truth. Real forgiveness does not imply that we excuse the insensitive or harmful acts of others; it simply means that we no longer allow them to dictate the course of our lives.

It has been said many times—in many languages and in many ways— that, in the greater scheme of things, we are our own worst enemy. The first step toward forgiveness must be directed within. Only by embracing the lightness that comes with forgiving ourselves for our flaws, mistakes and shortcomings will we progress in our journey toward successful inner healing.

Chapter 3: Affirmations
I accept new perspectives, I perceive new horizons

- I have clarity within myself; I consider other perspectives.
- I will no longer sabotage my present or future because of false self-perceptions from my past.
- I observe the patterns in my life, as they indicate the path I must take to heal my own world.
- My perception is expanding and I see a brand new life opening up in front of me.

Chapter 3: A Taste of the Spiritual Unknown

Since ancient times the snake has been associated with change and renewal. Because it periodically sheds its skin, this wondrous reptile has been the object of spiritual worship and reverence in many cultures. With the advent of patriarchal religions, and the desperate attempt to eradicate matriarchal systems of belief, many of the sacred symbols were demonized and falsely associated with images of evil and deception. This was the beginning of purposefully corrupted perceptions and interpretations, with the intention to control through fear.

In ancient times, the West African Voudou tradition of Obi or Obeah, also known as the worship of Ob, was revered as being the most powerful tool of connecting with the Self. Ob is the primordial and cosmic serpent dwelling in the sky, whose twin image wrapped around a cross is often the symbol used by the medical community to represent all that is connected to healing.

In Kundalini Yoga, Ob is depicted as a coiled snake of powerful energy which resides at the bottom of the spine and remains dormant unless awakened suddenly by physical trauma to the tailbone, by erroneous stimulation through excessive mental exercise, or through imbalance of sexual energy. Once the Kundalini energy is properly released under the watchful eye of a trained teacher, its life energy rises through the seven Chakras (the seven stairs to God's Heaven) and flows smoothly until it connects to the Crown Chakra, therefore fusing with the celestial energy coming from the Cosmos. Once the two forms of energy are finally united, the powerful energy of Obeah is created.

In the Voodoo pantheon, the energy of the cosmic serpent is represented by Damballah.

Damballah is pure, its energy reflected in the white color which represents its essence. Worshippers of Damballah wear only white garments and maintain their area of worship pristine and free of chaos. He accepts only pure gifts, favoring anything white, such as white eggs, milk and coconut, and is the only Orisha who was never incarnated as a human before his status was granted. His power resides in his pure and gentle wisdom, with the unconditional love of the Heavens; his essence has been associated with the purity of the Christ.

Damballah is invoked mostly for healing of the mind and to seek help in removing the psychological blocks that hinder the progression of our Soul journey.

When a practitioner asks Damballah for help in overcoming blocks, he or she must be extremely respectful and aware of Damballah's high status in the hierarchy of the Orishas.

As seen with Elegba in the previous chapter, working with Damballah also warrants having complete faith and acceptance of the way things will unfold and the manner in which he will choose to arrange healing for the greater good of all.

Chapter 4

Closets and Attic
The Hidden Recesses of Our Minds

The mind is its own place, and it itself can make a heaven of hell,
a hell of heaven.
John Milton

Cleaning closets is synonymous with procrastination. It's a daunting task, one put off with a million excuses: We're too busy, nobody looks in our closets, we might need those things one day! We keep shoving things into our closets, not taking time to see what can be brought out for use, what we can get rid of, or what we can take up to the attic for safekeeping.

We deal with our cluttered closet situation only when we can't find something or when the contents reach critical mass.

The most dreaded aspect is the mess inevitably created before things are organized. Who wants to deal with that? As long as the mess is out of the way, we don't have to look at it. As we pull things out into the open, it will no doubt trigger memories we're not ready to face and questions for which we still may not have answers.

The attic is our really, really big closet. Guests never go into our attic; for that matter, *we* rarely go into our own attic. When you think about it, most people only venture into the attic during or after significant life changes: births, deaths, weddings, divorces, and relocation.

Consider that within each of us is found a closet (our conscious mind) and an attic (our subconscious mind). The process of organizing closets and the attic is the same required to bring healing to our lives.

First we'll focus on our conscious mind, the everyday closet of our lives.

The closet is where we try to organize commonplace items, things we might need yet don't want out in the open. Most of us start off with nice, neat closets, but as time goes on we tend to throw things in quickly and haphazardly; we keep adding, nothing is removed. It may take years, but our messy closets will one day result in tremendous frustration. It usually happens when we're in a rush and can't find something. As we move things out of the way frantically looking for the item in question, suddenly we aren't able to control the chaos; things begin to tumble out and the door can no longer be shut.

At that point we are forced to acknowledge the mess in the closet. It's time to do something.

The same is true of our thoughts. Every day we have a multitude of experiences and interactions, with corresponding thoughts and feelings. Thus far, all the thoughts and emotional charges connected with our daily experiences have been thrown together, unsorted, creating confusion. We never take the time to organize our emotional world.

One of the reasons our conscious mind becomes so cluttered is that we don't take time to process our daily thoughts and emotional responses, nor look at the important lessons within each experience. We fear being seen as unstable or silly if we react openly and honestly in many situations. Most of us have been trained from an early age to control our emotions and keep them under wraps.

Indeed, it is wise to learn to control one's emotions. However, controlling one's emotions and stifling them altogether are two different things.

Also, it's essential to our well-being to ensure that what we're sorting through is our own "stuff". Sometimes our closets can contain others' belongings. They come over to visit and accidentally leave something behind, so we put it in the closet and eventually forget to whom the item belongs.

Throughout our lives we are exposed to the opinions and beliefs of those around us, as well as their emotional dramas. After a while, it's easy to blur the boundary between what belongs to us and what has rubbed off from someone else and found a home in our internal closet.

The closet, our conscious mind, is mostly associated with "left-brain activity" and relies on sensory perception to gather the information necessary for the rational thinking process. It is also associated with the ego and is therefore easily influenced by physical sensations. Because of this limitation, perception can be contaminated by inner and outer pollutants, subconscious triggers, and external stimuli.

Remember the white noise we spoke of in Chapter Two? What we watch on television, what we read, what we hear on the radio, what we chat about with others, what we overhear...it all gets mixed together and becomes part of our internal white noise.

Seldom, if ever, do we take the time to sort through all of the information we're bombarded with each day or evaluate how we feel about it.

We humans are complex, so trying to understand ourselves can be quite intimidating and exhausting. There are many variables affecting how and why we respond the way we do. What is upsetting or joyful to one person can be the opposite for another. Indeed, what upsets us one day may not affect us whatsoever the next. Much of it has to do with the perceptions and perspectives which underlie so much of our human experience. Without realizing it, this can change frequently based on the situation, our mood at the time, etc.

I encourage you to be brave and get to know yourself. Now that you have created the space and time to quiet your mind, don't allow the clutter to keep piling up in your consciousness.

Start by simply not adding to the clutter for a few days. You don't need to drag everything out and sort through it quite yet, just don't add to it. Take a few minutes each day to be aware of your thoughts, reactions, and subsequent emotions. Sort it out first; don't shove it indiscriminately into the closet.

And, remember: Make sure they are *your* thoughts and emotions. Walk through them and detach from anything not yours.

While closets tend to be more for "what if" storage—things you think you might need at a moment's notice—attics are for family heirlooms, mementos of special events, and items we feel may be needed later in life or could be of value one day.

Sorting through the attic requires commitment. Our life history is in the attic, as are the histories of loved ones. It requires time to go through the memories and memorabilia. Unlike the closet's more casual everyday contents, intense emotions are often attached to the attic's treasures: photo albums, diaries, portraits, children's artwork, greeting cards, love letters, antique furniture and décor. It is a bittersweet task as we uncover memories which bring us joy and laughter, sadness and longing. We may discover things we can finally part with; on the contrary, we may find something we want to take downstairs and make use of in our daily lives, bringing it into the light of day.

Our subconscious mind is the attic within the house of our soul. It is the sum total of our experiences in a lifetime (some would say many lifetimes), and it is here where our most profound memories are tucked away—or buried.

What we feel, think, or do forms the basis of our experience which is in turn stored as subtle impressions in our subconscious mind. These impressions interact with one another and result in our tendencies to react in a particular way to a certain situation or stimulus. The reaction varies according to the character and temperament of the individual.

The subconscious mind is associated with our "right-brain activity" and is the home of our creative nature. It is also where our instinct and intuition reside. Unlike its conscious counterpart, the subconscious mind is not limited at all; however, there are some things we cannot comprehend within the current constraints of human consciousness.

It encompasses two overall functions: storage of information filtered through the conscious mind and soul-level guidance.

The subconscious mind is a very humble and conscientious worker, seldom questioning the information sent along by the ego. It makes itself known by occasionally knocking gently on the door of our intuition. If we don't hear the knocking or choose not to open the door, the subconscious mind holds its peace and accepts the decision of the conscious mind.

Not listening to the protective nudges of the subconscious mind often leads to unpleasantness.

Several years ago I met a woman I didn't like from the moment I laid eyes on her. I had the instinctive feeling this person was not trustworthy and felt uncomfortable having her around my family and within my immediate personal space. Because of social demands, her presence slowly increased and soon invaded my life. My conscious mind worked overtime trying to convince me that I had been wrong in my original assessment. I began to wonder if I had jumped to conclusions, as I am not comfortable standing in judgment, so I welcomed this person even closer into my life. She appeared genuinely sweet and kind; however, it was not long before her true colors bled through the veneer. She caused my entire family a lot of grief that could have been avoided had I followed that gut instinct.

That's how the subconscious sends its suggestions: a very light punch in the stomach and the lingering sensation that something is not right, although we can't quite put our finger on it. If not acknowledged, this subtle feeling can easily be drowned out by our rational mind and the thoughts formulated by the ego.

There are many books and studies regarding the conscious and subconscious minds, how they work individually and in tandem, and how we can manage their functions. If this subject is of interest to you, I encourage you to delve into it more deeply. For our purposes here, we will keep our focus on simply being aware of the two minds at work within each of us, and why it's critical we include the closet and attic as we clean and organize the house of our soul.

We must take charge of our closets and attic, know their contents, and sort out what to keep and what to release. Until we do, they control our daily lives in more ways than we can imagine. When they are clean and organized, we can better manage how we respond to situations and take a more intentional creative role in crafting our lives.

The two separate minds are always at work inside each of us. Although they work in unison toward the common goal of manifesting thoughts into reality, each is capable of processing — and creating — independent from the other.

Many wonder how dreams fit in with what we store in our conscious and subconscious. In my opinion, dreams are a dance between the two minds. The conscious mind uses the dream state to analyze impressions and unresolved feelings, while the subconscious mind sends symbols of guidance.

It is my personal experience that the subconscious guidance dreams are clear and flow as though watching a movie, whereas the conscious mind's "sorting" is broken down in little pieces that don't seem to be related in any way. The subconscious messages are not related to immediate experiences or events; the conscious messages are always related to something going on in my life at that moment.

There is a plethora of books and articles based on studies which have shown that thoughts stored within the subconscious mind manifest in our daily lives (and dreams). One of the tools the subconscious mind uses within the creative manifestation process is to measure the emotional charge attached to a thought. Without the fuel of the emotional charge, a thought is just a thought, a mere image that might have been sent mistakenly.

The emotions tied to our thoughts are one of the most powerful indicators of the reality we are passively creating. Imagine if we were to *intentionally focus* on an emotion in conjunction with an image of what we are calling forth into our lives (creative visualization), how very powerful that creative tool would be.

Certainly there are other factors beyond our current ability to comprehend which contribute to the reality we experience. However, it is my firm belief, as well as the belief of spiritual masters throughout time, that thoughts have energy; intentional thoughts, supported by emotion, have creative energy.

As we continue to clean our house, we will take a closer look at this concept and use it to create the experience of our choosing.

Consider that at each crossroads in our lives, both minds suggest a course of action; the subconscious mind sends guidance through feeling, while the conscious mind sends its own "logical" guidance.

The choice of guidance we will follow is entirely our choice, but the best path to walk is usually the one in the middle. We should carefully consider conscious choices that are accepted within the boundaries of the society we inhabit, but we should also accept the pure suggestions of our inner guide, for it rarely leads us in the wrong direction.

When we consciously give ourselves permission to heal and start listening to that inner voice, we show respect for both minds at work. We must accept the fact that both minds exist to do our will, and honor both for their part in creating the life and the person we have become thus far. By respecting both minds and showing gratitude for and awareness of their mutual existence, we open the door for a new team effort, working in unison toward the achievement of a new goal.

People are always surprised when I suggest giving themselves permission to heal but are amazed by the progress made once they embrace this simple concept. When you express gratitude for what has been, accept where you are, and give yourself permission to create a more joy-filled life, it is as though a tremendous weight is lifted from your shoulders.

With this in mind, we can now explore whether there are any items previously stored that we can discard.

Much of the content filling our minds is simply clutter amassed through negligence or inattention. Some of this information seems irretrievable since it was stored so long ago, but it can be brought into the open as we gradually make our way to the quiet caverns of our soul.

Our lives are a mirrored reflection of all that goes on inside of us; by observing the patterns in our world, we can see what we need to work on. If we look closely, we can also see how harmful patterns were created by listening only to our rational mind and ignoring our intuition. If we are wise, we will learn to listen to both.

The human drama of good versus evil, logic versus intuition is as old as time itself. We are familiar with the image of a person in the midst of having to make a choice, with an angel on one shoulder and a devil on the other. The battle between the conscious mind and subconscious is the basis of this classic human struggle.

A few years ago, I met a very interesting woman at the local flea market and was immediately attracted to her energy. I delighted in talking with her, and often went there on Sundays when I knew her booth would be open.

One day she asked me how well I had listened to my inner guidance throughout the week and then said, "You have to listen very carefully sometimes, because God only whispers but the Devil is very loud."

That statement made so much sense!

Most of the sacred books we are familiar with depict a mighty God and a wretched, evil creature at war with one another.

Although I am certainly not a religious expert, I have studied several different paths to see that they all share a pattern. The name by which Spirit or "God" is referred changes according to each tradition and is portrayed as the Almighty Source of all energy, the Alpha and the Omega, the beginning and the end of all things. In some traditions there are other high entities such as saints and angels working with God to lead the deeply-flawed human onto the path of righteousness, stopping him from being swayed by the Devil.

The Devil is depicted as a monstrous being, sly and deceitful, always lurking in the shadows and ready to steal the soul of believers gone astray.

In all religions, God and the Devil are forever at war, and their very distinct paths are always splitting in front of the human, who is often conflicted about which road to follow.

God and the Devil offer different rewards: God's blessings take time and patience to reach but are more fulfilling, while the Devil promises an instant but short-lived reward. God offers eternal life after death, and the Devil markets his goods as being enjoyed instantly in this life.

This conflict is at the base of all religious teachings.

If we step back and take a closer look at the two minds, the conscious and subconscious working inside each of us, we can see the same pattern. The subconscious mind is the mind of God, eternal and omniscient, never pushing anyone into a corner but merely suggesting a course of action through feeling. The conscious mind is the mind of the Devil, always ready to control our choices with the use of fear, as well as appeal to the desire for instant gratification. It is connected to survival of the body, rather than the well-being of the soul, and takes every possible chance to push us, at times aggressively, to make ego-based choices.

In the "Book of Genesis", Adam and Eve are portrayed as completely content in the Garden of Eden, living off the gifts of God and with no worries encumbering their souls. Once the Devil (the conscious mind or ego) slyly suggested to Adam and Eve to eat the apple of knowledge (rational, left-brain guidance), the magic was broken and the two poor souls were cast away, separated from their connection with God (the subconscious mind).

At any given time in our lives, we are never alone. Our ego pushes for us to feel disconnected and out of touch, but if we pay close attention we realize our feelings of isolation are only an illusion. If we patiently and diligently watch for signs and remain open to messages, something will happen which will offer guidance.

Guidance can come wrapped in many guises. It could be in a random situation we witness, in a television or radio commercial, or even in one of the many flashes of thoughts that cross our minds after we have been wondering about something.

No matter how the guidance reaches us, we must remain available and alert if we hope to receive them. Furthermore, we must allow ourselves to trust the guidance which comes from deep within. If we belittle its importance or dismiss the voice as "silly imagination", we limit our vision and narrow the scope of our understanding. We limit our potential.

The Universe, Spirit, God...whatever name you prefer...is ever ready to provide answers and guidance, but it is very subtle, working through intuition and signs. As the wise lady at the flea market also offered, "The Devil (our ego) is very loud, and to hear the soft voice of God (our inner guide) we must listen very carefully."

The choice to accept or dismiss the guidance we receive is up to us; some of us will pay attention, while others will ignore it in favor of concrete, rational, even science-only approaches to life.

It is important to acknowledge the existence of our innate wisdom and respect it as guidance benevolently bestowed upon us by the greater mind which humbly and silently observes.

Intuition is our lantern in the darkness of illusion; by following its light, we can overcome even the greatest obstacles and remain true to ourselves. By accepting its guidance we can take one more step toward a boundless consciousness and one more step toward our highest potential.

There are so many surprising, helpful treasures to be found as we clean out the closets and attics of our homes, from small functional items which make everyday life easier to priceless possessions which remind us where our true riches are to be found. As we delve into these areas we will discover hidden resources, some of which may make our lives easier or more fulfilling. It is possible we'll discover things which make us cringe or trigger negative emotions within us, but we learn so much about the course of our lives in the process. Only when we are able to see something in the light of day, can we consciously decide whether or not it is worth keeping.

It is a quest on many levels when we dive into our home's closets and attics. Similarly, diving in to the closet and attic within us is an unearthing process, one beset with challenges and obstacles intertwined with delightful discoveries.

Although it is a difficult step within our *Housekeeping for the Soul* to-do list, we must be thankful for the blessings to be gained from this stage of "spring cleaning" and personal growth. When we remove these more demanding experiences and emotions from the depths of our awareness and bring them into the light, we can see them in their entirety. Only then can we look at them with our hearts and minds, with a fresh, newly integrated perspective and with one goal: Our personal journey toward wellness, toward wholeness.

Chapter 4: Affirmations
I release the challenges of the past and make room for my future

- I am a perfect expression of the subconscious mind of all creation.
- I make time to process my daily thoughts and emotional responses.
- I honor my intuition and heed its guidance.
- My thoughts have energy; intentional thoughts, supported by emotion, have creative energy.

Chapter 4: A Taste of the Spiritual Unknown
In keeping with our discussion of the conscious and subconscious minds, I have always found it fascinating that indigenous religions have a strong awareness of duality and balance. They see their lives as a perfect fusion of humanity and spirituality, and are intrinsically aware of the roles of the ego and soul...and the need to balance the two.

Most ancient peoples recognized and prayed to a god or goddess, or Spirit, and developed practices and rituals to create a bridge between the earthly world and the spiritual world. They often did so through the symbolic use of masks.

Masks are one of the most remarkable manmade creations used in rituals throughout recorded history, used by our ancestors to form a bridge between themselves and the Divine. Though in modern times the mask has a negative connotation of disguise with the intent to deceive, the ancient world perceived masks as tools of revelation, a connection to invisible powers. The human desire to know the unknown is given shape by ceremonial masks, revered in all ancient cultures.

As one continues on their spiritual journey into the unknown, the importance of balance becomes part of the unfolding.

In Voodoo, the most important entity when one thinks of balance is the mighty warrior, Orisha of balance and justice: The Great Shango.

Shango is known as Zeus in the Olympian pantheon and as Jupiter in Roman mythology.

Regardless of the specific name this deity is assigned, he is the keeper of the scales that weigh the administration of cosmic justice.

Shango's colors are white and red, and he is associated with the electrical charge in the lightning bolt. He is a warrior who removes obstacles for the righteous but should not be summoned to obtain favors that go against the laws of mankind and Spirit.

When a practitioner asks for Shango's help, the best time to start the prayer is on a Thursday at midday, when the power and clarity of the sun are at the strongest point. He is said to love offerings of rum, green bananas, cigars, palm oil, beans, hot peppers, and anything that is masculine. A favored way to summon Shango is by lighting one red candle and one white candle, with a glass of water in the middle. When Shango arrives, his presence is fairly obvious, as the room temperature usually raises a few notches.

Chapter 5

Gifts
Finding the Blessings

Life is raw material. We are artisans. We can sculpt our existence into
something beautiful, or debase it into ugliness. It's in our hands.
Cathy Better

Now that we understand the importance of having more organized, functional closets and attic space, we must decide what to do with what has been brought into the open for inspection and sorting. This was what we have dreaded all along.

Everything is out in the open creating a mess, so we must gather our strength and stay focused on the task at hand. At this point it would be self-defeating to throw things back into hiding.

Let's take a deep breath and focus on one pile at a time.

The hardest part is deciding what stays and what goes. For the items to which we have emotional attachments, it's as though they carry a small piece of us, so it's hard to say goodbye. Even items which are attached to a negative memory are at times difficult to part with, perhaps due to guilt or a fear of breaking the connection to our identity of misery and pain.

Special consideration should be given to items received as gifts, as they are a direct link to the person who gave them to us, including when we gift ourselves.

Let's start the sorting process by taking all of the gifts received through the years which ended up in the closet and attic and placing them in one big pile.

Throughout our lives we receive many gifts and can feel guilty at the thought of getting rid of these items; it feels disrespectful in some way. Depending upon the nature of the gift and the relationship to the giver, it can even feel like a betrayal.

The plain truth is that many of these gifts no longer fit our lifestyle or our personal preferences, and they're taking up a lot of space we could use for things of our choosing.

Much could be said about the blessings and curses bestowed upon us with each gift. We will see how some of these gifts made perfect sense at the time but are no longer relevant, and how other gifts were ignored but can now be put to good use.

In this chapter we will use the concept of "gift" to bring to light aspects of ourselves and our circumstances that have entered our world, sometimes without our invitation. What we traditionally label as a gift is something that has value and will bring us happiness, but the greatest gifts we receive are the hidden opportunities lying behind unwanted situations in our lives.

At one time or another most of us have received a gift from someone we're not particularly fond of. When this happens we can't wait to exchange the gift or toss it in a closet, out of sight. Sometimes these become part of the regifting cycle, usually given to another we're neither close to nor overly fond of.

Since it was received from a person who invokes a negative emotion within us, the gift is already tainted by our own judgment and perception. Even if it were a lovely or valuable gift, we would likely discard it based on who it came from.

Every gift we receive should be acknowledged with gratitude, no matter the source. By automatically dismissing it, we might deprive ourselves of something wonderful. There is no mistake made when something is given to us, as everything in the Universe works with perfect timing and perfect design, regardless of how things may appear. We receive exactly what we are asking for, whether the gift is in a form which elevates our spirit or crushes our ego. What influences what we receive is the hidden message behind what we ask for and how we ask for it.

Imagine a dear, elderly friend has recently hit the lottery. She isn't wealthy but is now financially stable, and she announces her plan to get you something special for your birthday. You know she will ask friends and family what you'd like, as she wants to surprise you yet has no idea what would be the perfect gift.

You do have a lavish gift in mind that you'd love. In fact, it's something you've dreamed about for a long time. However, although your friend can afford it without hardship, you are not comfortable asking for it. You don't feel deserving and are afraid to voice what others may see as a ridiculous and pretentious request. In your mind, you assume the request will be rejected, which will confirm that you're unworthy or selfish for asking.

In the end, when asked by others what you would like for your birthday, you suggest smaller, less expensive gifts which won't be seen as a burden. Rather than say what you truthfully desire, you ask for something less than…which is a direct reflection of how you see yourself.

It's a common pattern for so many of us. When we receive the gift we asked for, we are disappointed. Are we expecting others to be psychic and read our minds?

Your friend would have been more than happy to indulge your heart's desire, but she offered what she did because she thought it would make you happy. She thought it was what you really wanted.

If we are fortunate, we go through this process of gift giving and receiving numerous times during the course of our lives. Rarely do we receive what we truly want, because rarely do we express to others what that is!

This concept applies to every aspect of life, from personal relationships to careers.

Many years ago I worked in a hotel as a front desk clerk. After hearing through the grapevine that our reservations manager was ready to vacate her position, I began to express interest in taking her place. I helped her file hundreds of reservations, took her calls while she was at lunch, and did everything possible to learn her job as quickly and efficiently as possible. I assured the general manager that I would gladly *help*, and that I could easily *fill in while I still attended to my present position*. I wanted them to feel comfortable that I wouldn't abandon my current responsibilities, and hoped to bolster my professional image by stating that I loved the face-to-face interaction with the customers my front desk position provided.

The day the manager left came sooner than expected. Since I was the only person who knew what to do in the reservations office, I was told that someone else would take over my current position so that I could dedicate myself entirely to running the reservation office. I was ecstatic! I was certain the job was mine.

One morning, about two weeks later, I received a knock on my office door. A new girl excitedly informed me that she was the new reservations manager; to add insult to the injury, I was the one who was supposed to train her.

I was crushed. I was angry and felt I had been taken advantage of; I worked two jobs for one pay, only to be replaced by someone with no experience.

It wasn't long before I came to realize that no one had wronged me. After all, I had never clearly asked for the position. In fact, I stated quite clearly that I was glad to "help out." I had even made it a point to clarify that I loved face-to-face exchanges with the customers, something the reservations manager position did not offer.

The general manager hadn't really bypassed me. In all likelihood he was trying to be kind by allowing me to remain in the position I seemed to love. The perceived rejection was a gift and gave me the opportunity to open my eyes to my own lack of clarity in communications. Indeed, it wasn't the manager who thought that I was not qualified for the job; I was the one who questioned my own qualifications and didn't feel confident enough to come out clearly and state, "I would love this job, and I know I'm fully capable."

Subconsciously, my fear of being rejected led me to wear a mask that would make me appear humble and happy to have the job that I had. In the end, I received exactly what I asked for and believed I deserved.

We must remember to be honest with ourselves and state clearly what we desire in this life…say it to ourselves, to others who ask, and to the Universe.

As we continue to sort through the stack of gifts, we must decide whether or not we will ever use them. By pulling them out into the open, we are able to see them clearly and assess any place they may have in our Now.

Some of the gifts we have received were a good fit for us when first given but no longer fit the person we are today. As our perceptions shift continuously, so do our needs and desires. We may appreciate support during the course of a trying event, but the attention could feel invasive when the crisis is over. We must evaluate the gift in light of our current life situation and be strong enough to release it if there is no longer value. Again, we can remain grateful while also choose to remove it from our lives.

The most meaningful gifts we receive quite often come wrapped as tragedies and betrayals. When we come face to face with a conflict or crisis, we are too caught up in the unfolding drama to see the treasure or lesson. It is only in the aftermath that we can see the blessings bestowed.

It may sound trite, but it is through trials that we strengthen our character and develop virtuous qualities which otherwise elude us. When we pray for something, we must remember that it usually doesn't magically materialize in front of our eyes. Instead we will be given the opportunity to learn how to manifest it ourselves.

I remember years ago praying to be a good parent to my

children, certainly a more patient one. Almost immediately I found myself knee-deep in a string of situations that actually tried my patience to the breaking point. Annoyed and shaky in my faith, I questioned whether I was simply wasting my time with prayer. Only years later did I realize that prayers manifest in strange ways, mostly by providing opportunities that will teach us how to create and experience the very things for which we prayed.

Quite often we are provided with a contrast—we experience what we *do not desire to experience*—in order to clarify our intention and desire, as well as our commitment to achieving it.

The trying situations that I perceived as a curse while in the midst of them were indeed blessings in disguise. They increased my tolerance and patience, and provided me with a different scale to weigh the priorities of parenthood.

I have been fortunate to be able to see the gifts within each and every trying experience in my life, and have the ability to see the same for others. Throughout my life I have attracted those who have a pattern of tragedy. Because I am detached and can view their path more objectively than they, it is usually evident what pattern is occurring.

I am also blessed to be able to help others dig deeply to uncover the blocks resulting in the patterns, the process of which has led to the creation of this book. Certainly for traumatic experiences, time must pass and one must be open to seeing the treasures to be gleaned from the crisis they just endured. When they are ready, I am honored and humbled to help them uncover the gifts and lessons hidden within what was perceived as a tragedy.

I do not know of anyone who is fully aware and 100% certain of their true purpose in this lifetime. We embark on our journey the moment of our birth, unsure of the path that is laid out before us.

In her book, *Sacred Contracts*, Caroline Myss suggests that we have signed pre-birth contracts with other souls for the work we shall perform as we try to help one another in our soul evolution. According to Dr. Myss, we are all angels helping each other fly. Those who cause us grief, disappointment and heartache are crossing our path because we mutually agreed they would help us by being a catalyst for our inner growth.

An example of possible soul contracts at play, and another lesson in perspectives and gifts, comes through the story of Renee.

Not long ago several friends were discussing the concept of "creative visualization". Renee and I had shared several discussions about our spiritual paths, so I knew this concept was very familiar to her and that she believed thoughts have energy.

I was surprised by her reaction when someone mentioned how popular the "you create your reality" message had become. Most people, especially those who have explored various spiritual paths for decades, accept that statement rather straightforwardly without giving it much thought. Everyone in this group agreed with the statement without hesitation, except Renee.

Later, we all received an email with the following explanation. I am including it here with her permission:

Let me first say that I completely agree our thoughts have energy and thus affect our experience. However, I feel this definitive statement "you create your reality" is potentially self-defeating and possibly harmful. I believe it is wise to pay attention to our thoughts and recurring life patterns, but I also believe there are aspects at play beyond what most of us can currently understand.

To tell people who have intentionally focused on positivity for a long time that any negative experiences have been directly created by them is…cruel. It leads to guilt, and most of us have had plenty of that for several lifetimes.

I have a different point of view than most I know, and will tell you exactly why this oversimplified message of "you create your reality" disturbs me and, quite frankly, offends me at times, depending upon how it is presented.

I started exploring spiritual paths at an early age. I believed (and still do) that thoughts, with the power of intention, have energy. I immersed myself in activities and a lifestyle which supported this belief, always working to do better in thoughts, actions, and intentions.

I never imagined having children, but at 28 I was stunned to discover I was pregnant. When I got over the shock, I was delighted! I was blissfully happy those nine months! I did everything right: I was healthy, I was appropriately cautious when need be, I was bursting with love for this little soul. I talked to him nonstop and felt him move very early, at 10 weeks. I spent nine months completely immersed in envisioning and working toward wellness. That was it, a simple vision, not complicated, not greedy. I used my energy to focus on wellness for our little unit...wellness on all levels...spiritually, mentally, emotionally and physically. I believed I contributed tremendously to creating my reality and was consciously doing my very best to do just that.

I was full-term, ready to pop....so very excited to hold this little person and hear his voice.

Joshua was stillborn.

No warning. We'll never know what happened.

I don't blame anyone or anything. Perhaps it was a soul contract thing or Divine Timing...things I can't understand.

Sometimes a different path presents itself from the one we're so diligently trying to create. And it's not our fault. I know I didn't directly create the loss of Joshua with my thoughts or intentions, and it was hurtful to hear others say I did. I learned how very little control I actually have over many things.

I still do my best, always trying to do better to keep my energy funneled toward loving, joyful vibrations. And I also release it and allow, as my thoughts and energy can only do so much. That is my personal belief.

I immediately saw the perfection in what he gifted me with: unconditional love. Don't get me wrong, the pain was devastating, for many years. I became afraid to let go of the pain at one point. It was as though it was my last connection to Joshua...I identified with the pain so strongly. But I got beyond that, thank goodness.

What this taught me, personally, is that because our realities are intertwined with others' realities, sometimes things don't manifest as we picture it, no matter how well we do the "create our reality" thing.

Some things simply are.

In the case of Renee and Joshua, perhaps we can step back and evaluate it and identify it as most likely a soul contract having played out in this case. Some might say it was Renee's focus on wellness which resulted in Joshua departing; perhaps it was Joshua's soul contract to enter this world with what would be perceived as a disability or somehow unwell, and it was therefore a soul-level conflict.

What we all took away from reading her story is this: The "why" or "how" doesn't always matter. When there is no pattern involved, sometimes there is nothing to understand. We can accept the beauty and pain and everything offered in the experience without having to understand it. It just is.

So, it is time to be honest with ourselves. For each object we pick up, we must decide whether we will ever have any use for it again or perhaps it can be an heirloom to pass on to a loved one. If not, we can treasure the memory and be grateful for what it provided, but we must also be willing to part with it if it is taking up too much space. We must be committed to removing anything we have kept through a sense of guilt, obligation, or any other ego-based tendency.

Once we make a conscious choice to eliminate the old, we must start with a clean slate and be willing to remove all items which continue to trigger any negative emotions within us. Only then can we move forward, keeping only those gifts which are an asset to our new life.

Letting go is difficult. Regardless of whether the gifts have a positive or negative impact, they have been a part of us, so we must honor ourselves as we undertake this cleansing process.

Be proud that you have the courage to bring it all out of the shadows and choose what shall remain and what must go. You are most definitely well on your way to reclaiming your authentic self.

While I do believe nearly everything that manifests in our lives has a purpose and a lesson found within, perhaps there are some gifts, such as Joshua's short-lived presence, which are to be accepted for their blessings, without trying to find the lesson involved.

As we hold the memories of our life's greatest tragedies and blessings close to our heart, it would be wise to consider that perhaps there are times when gifts are simply gifts, and we should learn to accept them with grace. At times what we need to let go of is the desire to understand the underlying meaning.

Sometimes the act of receiving with an open heart, without thought, is the perfect step in our evolution and the most profound gift of all.

Open that heavy front door and gladly accept the gifts for your soul, and be thankful.

Chapter 5: Affirmations

I am thankful for the blessings hidden in all that was, for they led to what is

- I open my heart and welcome gifts for my soul.
- I call forth my soul's desires; I take time to be clear and intentional in my communications and prayers.
- Once I see the blessing, I release anything I choose not to accept into my life.
- I am open to seeing the gift within recurring painful situations.

Chapter 5: A Taste of the Spiritual Unknown

Ritual gifts or "offerings" are often looked down upon by modern society. This is primarily due to the lack of knowledge regarding the rituals as far as their history and intentions. As we have seen, lack of knowledge creates fear and humans tend to fear the unknown.

While most people envision ritual offerings as human or animal sacrifices used to "appease the gods", there is an entirely different type of ritual offering with an entirely different approach which goes back to the ancient times.

In Voodoo, various items are offered to the different Orishas according to what the Orisha is said to be attracted to energetically. The reason behind this practice is that, by offering a gift to the Orisha, you are gifting that part of your true self which will materialize your wish. This is why the choice of offerings is left to the individual, as it is important that he or she also be attracted to the offering energetically or feel it is appropriate in some way according to the wish.

The ultimate unknown for our human, earth-bound mind is death. However, in most cultures there has always been a direct correlation with birth, be it in the afterlife or through reincarnation.

Largely because they have been grossly misunderstood, many of the most feared entities around the world and throughout time are those spirits associated with death.

A popular spirit revered in New Orleans is that of Maman Brigitte, the bride of Baron Samedi and the keeper of graveyards.

Brigitte's colors are purple and black and her number is 9; her association with this number is very significant, as it is considered a number of finality.

Because of her connection to death, Maman Brigitte is also associated with rebirth. If we extend our exploration to the mythical world of Tarot, the card of Death (#13, the number of renewal) is a symbol of rebirth.

The gifts favored by Brigitte are eggplant, hot peppers, strong liquor that can warm her bones, purple flowers, fruits and vegetables.

In a very emotionally liberating ritual, previously-worn garments are brought to her, along with a selection of the above offerings. In the ritual, Brigitte is called upon to help in removing the old self in favor of giving birth to the new.

Chapter 6

Letting Go
Reduce, Reuse, Recycle

To be wronged is nothing unless you continue to remember it.
Confucius

We have sifted through the gifts received over the years and walked down memory lane...laughing, crying, feeling blessed, perhaps still feeling sadness or resentment.

With less clutter blocking our view, we can finally begin to envision the sanctuary we are creating.

The remaining items are now organized in neat piles, and it is time we take a deep breath and make final decisions: Should we trash them? Keep them? Donate them?

This is where things get tricky.

Some of the miscellaneous items were easy to dispose of, but when it comes to personal things we realize our attachment is stronger. There are physical memories attached to our clothing and accessories. They are the embodiment of the various stages of our lives, a perfect time capsule. As we stare at the many articles of clothing piled in front of us, we struggle to remain anchored in the Now.

Many of us still have favorite outfits from years ago, maybe decades, and would love nothing more than to be able to simply *fit* in them once again. But even if we could, would we really want to wear them now?

Here we will use the symbolism of clothes as the perfect reflection of the stages of our lives and how we use external imagery to express ourselves as unique individuals. As we begin to pull the old clothes from the pile—the old beliefs, perceptions, and opinions—we remember when we considered them quite fashionable. We recall buying them, or the people who gave them to us; we remember wearing them during certain events and who we were with at the time.

Certainly, we will come across items which make us cringe at the thought of having worn them at one time. *Good heavens, what was I thinking?!*

Our old clothes represent the image we were trying to impress on the mind of the outside world; they were the costume we wore, the mask which provided entrance into the play of daily life. At times we used to—and perhaps continue to—hide our fears behind the shield of our attire.

Our wardrobe can express to the world who we desire to be, or it can be a billboard for our feelings of inadequacy.

As children, many of us felt compelled to "dress up". By doing so we could become different people and create our own imaginary world. The little girl living in poverty could be a princess for an afternoon, and the little boy being abused could magically become the valiant police officer who *could* stop the bad guys. By wearing costumes and masks, we temporarily altered our imperfect reality.

Adults use image to manipulate reality as well. We dress in certain ways to prompt a reaction and wear certain clothes to display our moods. When the image we attempt to sell to the world does not match our inner view of ourselves, we feel awkward and send mixed messages to those around us.

Our image changes with each stage of our lives; we move on to different trends and styles, leaving a small part of ourselves attached to the costumes of our past.

Although we are sure we will never wear a particular outfit again, we might resist throwing it out. *What if it comes back into style?* In truth, even if it did, it would never quite fit us the same.

We act similarly with the different beliefs and emotional

attachments absorbed through the phases of our lives. Even if we could apply them to our present reality, we probably would not want to; we are different people now.

One would think that the process of cleaning and reorganizing our homes and lives would be exciting and greatly anticipated, but letting go of the past is like saying goodbye to the person we once were. This can be painful.

As we saw at the very beginning of this book, it is human nature to fear *any* change. No matter what wonderful surprises the future may hold, releasing our past means letting go of the security blanket of what is familiar.

Just as we must rid ourselves of things no longer needed or desired as we clean our physical homes, we must do the same as we tend to the housekeeping of our soul.

Emotions, memory fragments and attitudes attach to us through time; many of these no longer resonate and it is time to release what no longer fits. All that was forcefully or subtly thrust upon us by society, loved ones, or religion served a purpose when we accepted it in our lives, but it is now outdated and ill-fitting. By consciously removing everything which no longer has a place in our sanctuaries, we can finally begin to feel truly at home.

Not knowing what will happen next after we have let go of all that was creates inner turmoil; it is unsettling and stressful. But we also know that, without risk or at least being open to change, we won't come close to reaching our goals.

When I was young my mother had a favorite mantra that she freely dispensed anytime she heard of a successful venture: *money makes money.*

Those three words have stayed with me through the years, and I have rolled them through my mind countless times, not necessarily related to finances but to life in general. When I came to the States I heard variations of the same concept, namely *you have to spend money to make money.* The idea is that we must take a risk and invest in our dream if it is to come true.

Having inner confidence, inner knowing, or perhaps pure, unadulterated determination—if only for a brief moment in time—is required to dive into the unknown and take a chance. Yet some of the riskiest ventures have been openings to unprecedented success.

Most of today's successful online companies were a huge risk for their creators. Even the founders of business giants such as Amazon, E-Bay, and Google took on a tremendous margin of risk to launch these projects. Fortunately for them the explosion of home computer use fueled their businesses' growth beyond anyone's wildest dreams. However, they had no guarantees when they first started; they took a chance and leaped into the unknown.

Reflecting on something a little closer to home, my husband and his brother were both employed by others until eight years ago. They were unhappy with their work situation, so they began to talk about starting their own business. At the time my brother-in-law was single, but we had two children and mostly lived on my husband's income.

The whole idea was frightening and triggered thoughts of insecurity and doubt. At the same time, it was exciting. Taking a chance of that kind could mean two things: We could do well and improve our lives, or we could lose everything. Our chances were fifty-fifty.

The pressure on my husband was tremendous. He was extremely dissatisfied with his work and needed a change, but he also knew a step in the wrong direction could mean financial devastation. The hardest part was that he wasn't making this choice solely for himself; he knew that he was also responsible for a wife and two young children.

Every time we talked about it, we felt as if we were stranded on an abandoned ship slowly sinking into the ocean. We had a chance to board a flimsy raft, but that meant facing storms and unknown dangers at sea in a weak vessel. On the other hand, remaining on the ship would lead to our certain demise.

A decision had to be made, and we were terrified. We took a leap of faith and hopped on the flimsy raft.

We invested the little money we had in the purchase of a used tow truck and proceeded to become a legitimate business entity providing towing services. My husband and his brother left their secure-though-disheartening jobs and focused solely on getting the new business up and running.

After a few months of working nonstop for very little money, they were almost ready to give up. That's when an unexpected opportunity presented itself. One of their clients, the owner of a service station, had recently experienced serious medical problems and was considering selling his business. Taking another risk, they quickly reached an agreement and decided to buy the service station themselves. The deal was arranged in less than a month. Since they didn't have the money, they had to borrow from friends and family, promising to pay everyone back with interest. The paperwork was drawn up, the necessary funds came through, and the deal was sealed.

As I think back on that first year, it all seems a blur. Money was tight, business was not flourishing, but somehow everyone was paid back. We bought two more businesses not long after and sold them for a profit. We sacrificed quite a bit those first few years, financially and otherwise, but everything worked out beautifully.

Today, only eight years since the initial thought of becoming self-employed, we are living a life we could not have hoped for prior to making the big change. We are not rich, but we are comfortable, and profoundly grateful for having the courage to take a chance.

Throughout history, there are many stories of success achieved by diving into the unknown. One of the most well-known and amazing examples comes to us from the explorers and founders of what is now the United States of America.

Before the first explorers decided to cross the Atlantic Ocean, it was believed that the Earth was flat and nothing was beyond the horizon. It was common to hear tales of boiling waters and terrifying sea monsters lurking in the deep, ready to overthrow any daring sea captain who was foolish enough to undertake such an impossible venture.

Against all odds, ready to forfeit their lives in the pursuit of knowledge and adventure, those first brave souls took their own leap of faith and discovered new worlds previously uncharted.

We can travel uncharted territories of our own once we decide to release fear and embrace the pure potential before us. As we gradually let go of all things which no longer serve us, we will find we have a much lighter load to carry as we move forward. Perhaps roads and vistas previously unseen will appear before us. We are so accustomed to taking the same route, with the same routines and scenery, that we get lost within the *sameness*.

It's easy to get lost in the patterns of our lives.

To fully heal and be able to let go, we must literally retrace our steps along our journey thus far and see the roads we have taken repeatedly, roads which have led to despair.

To explain this concept further, I would like to introduce Cynthia.

When I met Cynthia, she was in the process of leaving her husband. She immediately shared that he was physically abusive and had battered her time and time again. As I listened to her story I was appalled and, even though I really didn't know her, quickly tried to set things in motion for her to leave the abusive situation. Cynthia eventually went along with my suggested plan and left her violent husband.

One night while we were discussing her experience, she informed me she had been through four physically violent relationships, each escalating in intensity from one to the next.

Hearing this, I carefully asked about her childhood. She

confessed that as a young girl she witnessed violence on a regular basis. On many occasions she had seen her parents fight, inevitably ending with her father striking her mother.

As a small child her parents were her world. She adored them both for the roles they played: she loved her mother and wanted to imitate her goodness and patience, and she loved her father as well though struggled to understand why he was so angry toward his wife. Meanwhile, she felt she was in the middle, being pulled. She felt responsible for their fighting, which was consistently triggered by lack of money and personal space.

Cynthia admitted that, since her teenage years, she was always attracted to "strong" men who could be good providers, men who reminded her of her father. Although he was a violent man with frequent bouts of irrational rage, in her child-like mind her father was a good provider. It was her belief that a man with the same characteristics would take care of her.

Her desire to emulate her mother played a role in her life pattern as well. She saw her mother as a saint who endured the hardship of a perilous marriage for the sake of keeping her child's world safe and intact. Cynthia admired her mother's sacrifice and selflessness.

When she noticed the connection between her own relationships to that of her parents, something shifted inside. It was painful for her to talk about the times she had witnessed their fighting, but after reliving her pain and realizing she need not be abused to emulate her mother's gentle character, Cynthia released a huge burden. She also saw there was no logical connection between a man being a good provider and being prone to violence; this was the faulty perception of a young mind trying to make sense of what she could not understand.

Cynthia immediately initiated many changes in her life, starting with the conscious decision to love herself more. Prior to this inner exploration, she could not see the pattern. Indeed, she didn't know there *was* a pattern. Once aware, and with gentle guidance, she realized she could begin to manifest healthier, more loving experiences and relationships in her life.

There are times when we find ourselves standing at a crossroads; all too frequently we choose a direction, unaware that our sense of orientation is marred by our past. The paths we have chosen are influenced by the perception we have gained through countless relationships and events, compounded by the white noise which interferes with our intuitive navigational system.

Saying we can simply take a deep breath, start fresh and erase all thoughts of the past is unrealistic. Ultimately, we can't eradicate painful experiences from our past; even if we could, I suggest we instead view our past experiences as valuable lessons to be tucked into our treasure chest of wisdom. What we *can* do is understand the hidden triggers leading to the unwanted patterns in our lives by observing the circumstances we are living through today. We can't erase the past, but we can erase the emotional charge associated with the memories. We need not experience those same painful situations and types of relationships ever again.

It's time to let go of the emotional energy connected with the past, so that we can embrace our Now and anticipate an amazing future.

Are you ready?

Please join me and say the following out loud.

I lovingly release and let go of my old identity.
I let go of the pain.
I let go of the suffering.
I let go of the need to control.
I let go of guilt.
I let go of others' "stuff".
I let go of shame.
I let go of denial.

I let go of doubt.

I let go of fear of the unknown.

Release *all that was* so that all *that can be* may enter your life; enter the tunnel of the unknown and allow the light of your soul to finally shine through and show you the way.

Chapter 6: Affirmations

I release my past attachments and fear, for they no longer fit who I have become

- I release the fear that stops me from observing my emotions.
- I lovingly release and let go of my old identity; I release all that doesn't belong to me.
- I lovingly release pain, suffering, shame, denial, doubt, and guilt.
- I lovingly release the need to control.

Chapter 6: A Taste of the Spiritual Unknown

Another unknown for the vast majority of people in our modern world is the use of the word "magick".

Because of the mysterious cloak of fear which wraps itself around the word "magick", most people believe that only a few mysterious individuals hold the key to magickal manifestation. It is important to note that true magick is spelled with a "k" to differentiate it from stage magic.

There is no secret to magick. A thought is formulated, visualized, "felt" emotionally, and then *released* by the mind to Spirit. Release is the key element. By passing the worry to a Higher Power, one is then able to let go of the emotionality of the issue and focus on the more positive aspects of life.

Although it has been ostracized and demonized, magickal practice is nothing more than a highly-visualized prayer, very similar to those used by mainstream religions. The only difference between the two is that magick is "acted" rather than merely spoken.

Magick and Christianity and other organized religions are sister and brother who have not yet realized their family ties. Hopefully, as we open our hearts and minds to other beliefs and ways of life—broadening our perspectives—more and more people will come to understand that, at the core, the paths are very similar. No matter what our spiritual or religious affiliation may be, we all send wishes out to the Universe. Whether we address them to God, Allah, Kali, Aradia or Olodumare, the message or prayer is best served when released to the waiting hands of a Higher Power so that we can release the burdens weighing on our souls.

Chapter 7

The Family Room
Exploring Our Relationships

Almost all of our sorrows spring out of our relations
with other people.
Arthur Schopenhauer (18th Century German philosopher)

We've successfully cleared our home of unwanted clutter. What a tremendous accomplishment! The closets and attic are organized, and we no longer fear what may be concealed within, buried under years of avoidance and neglect. Once again, or perhaps for the first time, we are in command of our domicile and can breathe a sigh of relief.

Much earlier we created a small space where we could quiet our mind before undertaking this intensely personal renovation. We now have much more room; we can step back and envision our new living space. It is a blank canvas at this stage, waiting for our loving attention.

Let's sit in the family room and imagine what we'd like to do here. While the kitchen is often referred to as the heart of the home, the family room represents its soul.

When we think of a family room, the first image that usually comes to mind is that of a cozy, comfortably-furnished area, complete with loved ones and faithful pets all gathered together at the end of a long day. Our family room is where our most precious photos and keepsakes are displayed. It's where we laugh, cry, reminisce, and share words of love and encouragement.

In reality, this Utopian scene is more the exception than the rule. Seldom does the above scene play out in modern lives, though this idyllic vision remains.

How we personally view the family room is symbolic and often represents the parallel world of our relationships.

While growing up we entertain romantic thoughts of meeting our soulmate, forever dancing gracefully through the hazy ballroom of our fantasies. We imagine meeting the partner of our dreams; the prince who will sweep us off our feet or the damsel who forever sees us as her hero. When the veil of illusion is lifted and reality revealed, we see the prince is wearing a stolen crown and the princess has run off with the dragon.

In the beginning of a relationship, the stage of the delightful "butterflies", we feel as if we have finally met the perfect person for us. Rationally, we know they aren't perfect—but they are close to it early on.

It usually doesn't take long for our initial perception to falter. We start to notice the small flaws or habits that agitate us which we were blind to in the first stage of the affair. This inevitable course is such a predictable pattern in human relationships that it is recorded in an ancient Greek myth. The legend of Eros and Psyche is the story of a love affair, from the beginning to its fortunate end. While the popular tale is often told with slight variation, the crux of the story remains intact in each version.

Perhaps the same can be said of our relationships, with the same story essentially playing out and only the names changing.

Psyche was a beautiful princess. So beautiful that Aphrodite herself, the Goddess of Love, was jealous of her. Hoping to punish the mortal who had dared overshadow her beauty, Aphrodite sent her son, Eros, the God of love, to destroy her.

Aphrodite's plan was to send an oracle to the girl's father, warning him that great calamity was to befall his family and his land. He could avoid this if he agreed to take his daughter, Psyche, to a lonely rock in the middle of the sea where she would be sacrificed to a ferocious monster of the deep.

When Eros saw the girl, he was struck by her maddening beauty and accidentally pricked himself with one of the magic arrows used to make people fall in love.

Meanwhile, Psyche had accepted her dire destiny and surrendered. She waited patiently for the monster to come kill her and fulfill the oracle.

To her surprise, she was instead transported to a magnificent place where she was left alone until nightfall. Once the cloak of darkness had finally wrapped its velvety essence over all there was, Eros appeared to her. He told her that they were destined to be together. Although she could not see his face, Psyche was quickly hypnotized by his gentle demeanor and soothing words. Eros made her promise to never attempt to see his face. He kept her company by night, always disappearing with the light of the new day.

Psyche was happy with her unusual life, and was still able to visit with her family. Unfortunately, she could not ignore the cruel prodding of her two sisters. Both were angry and jealous of her bliss, and suggested repeatedly that she should take a look at her husband's face. One night while Eros was asleep, Psyche lit a lamp and placed it near her husband, hoping to finally see him.

When she realized that she was staring directly into the handsome face of Eros himself, Psyche was delighted but quite shaken. She accidentally dropped the lamp, spilling hot oil over him, causing Eros to instantly awaken. He reproached her for not having faith in him and his words, and then fled into the night.

Startled, she jumped back and pricked herself with one of the arrows, thus falling helplessly in love with the same man who fatefully swept her off the rock.

Everything around her disappeared, and Psyche found herself wandering around the world looking for her lost love.

After many trials were imposed giving her the opportunity to prove her love, Eros felt compassion for Psyche and asked Zeus for permission to be reunited with his beloved. Zeus consented, and Psyche was elevated to immortal status. From that moment forward, the two lovers were inseparable.

As in the legend of Psyche and Eros, we mere mortals go through this pattern of courtship, blind love, disappointment, and renewal. At the beginning of any romantic relationship, we see no flaws; we look through rose-colored glasses, unable to discern any imperfections. Once we get to know the person a little more, we realize they are not as perfect, nor as perfect for us, as we had originally believed.

At this point we struggle, trying to learn to deal with the facets of their personality which trigger negative responses within us. As time goes on, we either accept them as they are or decide to change course altogether.

The early years of a relationship are similar to a contract negotiation: We go in with great expectations that are, frankly, mostly selfish. We must listen to the expectations of the other party, put forth what is important for us, and then we are finally able to negotiate a satisfactory arrangement that both parties are willing to sign.

Modern statistics indicate that in nearly half of all relationships, the struggle ends in a loss, with the contract broken.

In our celebrity-obsessed society, we see couples coming together and breaking up in the blink of an eye, and this same pattern is witnessed all around us. The lack of longevity in relationships has become accepted, perhaps even expected.

In most cases the true reason for the breakup is never discussed in detail. Self-sabotage plays a larger role in the crumbling of relationships than anyone cares to admit. We blame our schedules, "where we are in our lives", and many other excuses, not wanting to examine the truth of the matter.

We've seen throughout this book how challenging it can be to explore our own lives. Many of us can't imagine going through the same grueling process with another. We must excavate two lives in order to get to the truth if we hope to have healthy relationships, but that is simply more work than most are willing to sign up for.

Imagine our home being in the messy state it was in before our success in sorting and letting go. Now imagine that we have a surprise guest arriving unexpectedly at our door.

Embarrassed by the conditions of our home, yet excited to have a little company, we receive them outside and try our best to conceal the mess hidden behind the front door.

We've been cooped up inside so long that the sunshine and gentle breeze make us feel alive once again. Talking to our guest energizes us for the first time in a long while.

We get lost in conversation and conveniently forget the mess we have behind the door.

Every day our surprise visitor comes back, and we look forward to the visits more and more each day. One day, our visitor asks to come inside. We politely ask them to please wait for a moment, as we make a mad dash through the house, throwing things back into the closet helter-skelter, throwing dishes into the dishwasher, shoving papers into the kitchen utensil drawer.

We spray some of the air freshener purchased ages ago to mask the musty odor and finally invite our visitor in. We are apprehensive that the mess of our lives may still be visible, yet excited to spend more time with our visitor.

The visitor notices immediately that the home isn't pristine but chooses to ignore it. The visitor enjoys our company and believes there must be a good reason why the house isn't tidy. In fact, the visitor is so inclined to like us that any scenario explaining why our home is a mess suffices.

After a few months, the visitor asks to move in. We have a moment of hesitation but quickly replace it with the comforting thought that we're loved just the way we are.

Once settled in, the visitor begins to notice the small things intentionally ignored before.

Suddenly, the crowded cabinets are frustrating, the stains on the floor stand out, the sink full of dishes is unnerving, and the clutter on the table is maddening!

While in the beginning we felt we had to hide our mess and our shortcomings, when we started living together we felt it was safe to be ourselves.

On the other hand, we were surprised when a lot of baggage was brought into our home unexpectedly; something the visitor neglected to mention. Having no place to put all of these belongings, the bags ended up in the middle of the floor, causing both of us to trip on them frequently.

Even through rose-colored lenses, the mess and obstacles and personal pet-peeves become painfully apparent, more than either could silently tolerate.

Rather than take a deep breath and work together to get things organized and tidy, the arguing begins. Each partner stands on opposite sides of the room, poisoned arrows in hand, ready to strike the other and blame them for everything, including the unfortunate fate of the relationship.

The same pattern takes place in relationships that are not of a romantic nature.

Most of us enter all types of relationships in a very step-wise fashion. We don't bare our souls or life history right away, as that would be odd. Instead, we present the side of us we want people to see as their first impression.

This would be fine if it wasn't for the human tendency to make assumptions based on casual impressions. Between the influence of varying perspectives and the illusive nature of initial impressions, it's very difficult to get an accurate portrait of someone. Once we have our impression, even if we encounter things to shift it over time, it's still very difficult to dislodge that original opinion of someone.

Another influence on these fledgling relationships is emotional triggers stored in our subconscious. For example, if we had a very negative experience with someone who had blue eyes and spoke with a certain accent, the next time we meet someone with these same traits we'll likely be turned off by them. Logically, we know there is no connection, but on an emotional level this has been programmed based on a past experience.

When we don't organize our internal closets and attic periodically, it's easy to see how the miscellaneous impressions and stimuli we absorb every day build to create flawed opinions and reactions toward others.

It is extremely common to see friends, siblings, and co-workers argue over pointless matters and trivial differences of opinion. Few people are ready to acknowledge their role in an argument, and small disagreements often escalate into unwarranted battles. It is like watching children bicker.

Observing my own children and their interactions teaches me so much about human nature.

After they've been instructed to clean their rooms, I'm always amazed how they easily become distracted and intentionally divert one another's attention. Of course, nothing is ever *their* mess; it's always someone else's. Likewise, while they believe they are working hard (though I have no idea how they can truly believe this!), in their minds no one else is doing their fair share in the cleanup process.

When I check on the progress, they remain fixed in place, glancing around at all that needs to be done yet taking no action.

I have often explained that each should worry about his own share, but the words never sink in. Ultimately, the time they spend complaining about the other's lack of resolve could be better spent working on the task at hand.

On a larger scale, this scenario is repeated on every stage in the theatre of human relationships. If something bothers us, we spend time and energy complaining about what others *aren't* doing rather than doing something productive on our own. I see this happening more and more frequently, about everything: politics, the economy, the education system, commerce, etc. Somehow we have become disengaged from doing anything about our problems; instead, it has become acceptable to complain and criticize, with no resolutions suggested or requested.

This negative thought process, without any attempt or desire to resolve the problems or concerns, has become the means to an end: Negative behavior gets attention. Children learn this early on, and we continue this behavior in a variety of ways, including portraying ourselves as helpless or besieged by life, especially to get the attention of those we love. We learn to use negative behavior to draw sympathy to our corner. As we continue with this negative persona and fully immerse ourselves in the role we have created, feelings of repression, limitation, anger, and sadness merge with our life energy, causing us to lose sight of the boundaries between our true identity and the mask of misery we have chosen to present to the world.

Many give the impression they're reaching out to connect with others, yet in many cases this is a surface image; secretly they hope no one responds, as this would reinforce the self-image of not being worth anyone's time.

It is exhausting to be around people who continually identify with all that is sad and hopeless in the world. Circumstances certainly lead most of us to feel this way at times. However, there are many who come to embrace this point of view as a lifestyle, not a transient mood based on a challenging situation.

Unless we have mastered the art of detachment, it is very hard to be around someone who repeatedly chooses to remain in a fog of misery without trying to work their way out. (Please note that I'm speaking of people who are fully capable of breaking this pattern, not those who are possibly in need of professional guidance for what may be clinical depression.)

For those who choose a life of misery because they don't feel deserving or because they've simply gotten lost along the way, eventually friends and family will decide they've had enough and leave them to their destiny. Of course, in the mind of the one now "abandoned", this confirms how little they are worth; as an added benefit, by being alone they are assured never to be hurt again.

One of my favorite stories revolves around the need for self-acceptance.

In a sad recall of her own life experiences, a woman spoke of the way others were always abandoning her or acting in a way which upset her life; one day, after taking the time to reflect on her multiple experiences of failure in the realm of relationships, she determinedly wrote down descriptions of their personalities and how they had failed her.

Amazingly, they all shared common traits—traits she was finally able to recognize as blocks she had within herself. This sudden awareness jolted her into action. She realized that the reason why others didn't like her was because she didn't like herself!

In the end, she made a very unique choice: she decided to "marry" herself. She did so with a playful ceremony in which she was both bride and groom. She asked for guidance in shedding the parts of herself that were going to sabotage the marriage, and vowed to love herself through the good and the bad. Rather than relegating her to a position of solitude, this newfound connection with herself enabled her to release the fears that consistently led her into devastating relationships. She made a choice to change the things she could change and to accept those she could not. Soon after, once she was no longer desperate to find a partner, the right person came into her life. Subsequent to her healing, the foundations of a good relationship were in place.

The lesson here is fairly obvious: Before we attempt to connect with others, we need to connect with ourselves.

The relationships in our lives, or lack thereof, offer a fascinating glimpse into the human psyche and the human experience. The types of people and situations we attract are often a mirror of the way we approach life. If we don't like the way someone behaves around us, then I strongly suggest we do something about it. Not to change them, but to change ourselves.

We will be amazed how the energy around us can shift when we notice within ourselves the very traits we dislike in others. It is my belief that we subconsciously, if not overtly, call forth relationships which will bring about our personal growth and help us learn more about ourselves.

Through others we are given the opportunity to heal ourselves.

Healing the relationships in our lives begins with identifying patterns reflected in the world around us which cause us emotional turmoil. If something deeply upsetting is presented to us repeatedly, it is time to understand why it is happening. What is it that we are trying to understand? What part of us is triggering this particular situation?

We will find that many of our relationships are simply role play aimed at justifying or understanding something in our past that we never dealt with, be it an issue of abandonment or a feeling of inadequacy. Once we identify the trigger, we can look through our personal catalog of past relationships to find similarities, work backwards to identify the cause of the emotional trigger, and then acknowledge and release it.

There are new lessons and opportunities for growth to be found within each relationship. As we have discussed, when there are negative patterns in relationships, it's time to get to the root cause creating this cycle.

Let us also keep in mind that relationships are often like gifts:

Some are simply meant to be treasured at face value, with no underlying lesson involved. In such instances, perhaps the only lesson to be learned is that of gratitude.

As you consider the importance and value of relationships throughout your life, and the types of relationships you would like to create and nurture, I leave you with one of my favorite quotes, from the artist, Flavia Weedn:

> Some people come into our lives and quickly go.
> Some people move our souls to dance. They awaken us to new understanding with the passing whisper of their wisdom.
> Some people make the sky more beautiful to gaze upon. They stay in our lives for awhile,
> leave footprints on our hearts, and we are never, ever the same.

Chapter 7: Affirmations
I let go of preconceived illusions of love, I accept myself and others

- I do not allow triggers hidden in my subconscious to corrupt my perception of relationships in my life.
- I focus my energy on what I can do to change a situation; I do not blame.
- I let go of self-sabotaging attitudes in order to build healthier relationships.
- As I learn to love and accept myself, the people I attract in my world are more receptive.

Chapter 7: A Taste of the Spiritual Unknown
When dealing with love and relationships, no deity comes to mind more than the beautiful Aphrodite.

As the embodiment of everlasting love, Aphrodite has been summoned since the times of ancient Greece to heal matters of the heart. Traditionally, Aphrodite, also known as Venus in the

Roman myth, was invoked to make someone fall in love or to bind two lovers together.

In those situations, gifts of her liking were brought near a body of water or to a temple dedicated to her, along with a work of magick crafted by one of her priestesses. Today people still venerate Aphrodite, and modern magickal practices still find their roots deeply embedded in these ancient traditions.

The most likely love spell would probably consist of pictures or objects belonging to the two lovers being bound together, facing each other, preferably with a coat of honey in between the pictures or objects.

Because she is the Patroness of Love, Aphrodite can also be summoned for matters of self love. That can be accomplished successfully by substituting the photo of the prospective lover with another picture of oneself. As we do that, tradition suggests that the practitioner will find true love for the spirit or God essence within. The idea is that when we fall in love with ourselves, we will attract others into our lives, including—but not limited to—a wonderful lover.

Chapter 8

Time to Clean!
Removing the Residue of the Past

You are responsible for your inner space; nobody else is, just as you
are responsible for the planet. As within, so without: If humans clear
inner pollution, then they will also cease to create outer pollution.
Eckhart Tolle

With our belongings finally organized and tidy, it's time to clean
our homes, from top to bottom, as we must start with a clean slate
before designing and decorating our new sanctuary. One can
only imagine the dust and grime and cobwebs that have formed,
layer upon layer, during the years of neglect. Even though we've
gotten rid of so many things that are no longer necessary, the
remnants of the mess remain.

The same is true of our inner world. We have succeeded in
working through a multitude of memories, triggers, and blocks
so we can move forward more freely in creating the life we
choose. However, the residue or imprint of those emotional
charges and attachments remains. It is time to get down on our
hands and knees and scrub, reach high and low into the corners
and crevasses of each room, all the while envisioning the
energetic release of all lingering vestiges of what we let go of in
Chapter 6: *pain, suffering, control, guilt, others' "stuff", shame,*
denial, doubt, and fear of the unknown.

As we dive into this task, I suggest we not view it as a chore;
rather, let's approach it as a multipurpose meditative exercise. We
can physically do these chores in the course of cleaning our
exterior residence, in whatever form that may take, while at the

same time doing the same symbolic cleaning within us.

Referring back to Elaine Klonicki's words at the very beginning of *Housekeeping for the Soul*, when you are vacuuming, see yourself "sucking up the cobwebs of less important thoughts so you can see your important ideas more clearly"; when you scrub the floors, set the intention to "scrub the floor of complacency, allowing your passions to shine through"; and when you clean the windows and mirrors, know you are "washing the windows into your heart and soul so they can speak to you more clearly".

Likewise, when you sweep the floor, know you are removing lingering particles of doubt from your path; when you take out the trash, know you are releasing all that you no longer need in your life; and when you wash the dishes, imagine cleansing your mind of any negativity that may have attached to your thoughts during the course of your day.

Also know that, while cleaning in this manner, you are exercising your body, mind and spirit. Try to enjoy it. Play music if that makes your heart lighter ~ dance and sing along! When you are done with the cleansing, then the exciting part begins: creating, designing and decorating the perfect reflection of you and all you desire.

In case I haven't convinced you that cleaning can be enjoyable and productive on many levels (believe me, I frequently must remind myself!), let me say that I completely understand the hesitation and outright dread at the thought of cleaning. Especially deep, intense cleaning.

The majority of experiences that led us to where we currently stand had a strong emotional charge attached to them. We've released the experiences themselves yet it is important to actively cleanse any damaging imprints from the intense emotions which have been with us for years, perhaps decades.

We resist this final step for the same reason many of us have allowed a thick layer of dust to collect on everything: When we start cleaning and dusting, the dust and dirt are stirred up and get into the air. If we just let the miniscule particles stay where they are, they aren't hurting anyone. After all, no one goes through our home with a white glove, so what's the harm?

The problem is, we know. We act carefree and nonchalant about our home being a mess, but it nags at us. Most of us have accepted that there is simply too much going on in life to have a perfectly *neat* home, but we are silently ashamed if we don't have a *clean* home.

Similarly, we allow the residue of past emotions to remain without cleansing and purging them. Again, the problem here is that *we* know; deep down inside we know there is an energetic imprint of these negative emotions which is still part of us.

This resistance to difficult cleaning tasks (both literal and figurative) can also be compared to the concept of a flesh wound. Many would consider the process we just went through—the excavation of painful, blocked memories and lifetime patterns— as having opened a gaping wound. Once we stopped the bleeding (acknowledging the experiences and the pain), a scab started to form as we went through the steps of letting go and releasing.

At this point we are once again afraid that, if we pull back the scab, the wound will freshly bleed again.

The concept of allowing a wound to heal is certainly desirable, but we have to make sure the wound is clean. If, under the scab, there is the potential for infection which could spread throughout our entire system, it is advisable to clean the wound. Even if overt health problems do not arise, it is well known that toxins (and emotional baggage) drain us on a physical and mental level, leaving us feeling sluggish and uninspired.

In addition, emotional stress is now known to be a cause of physical illness.

We have already undertaken the most difficult steps in the

process of our inner healing. Now, it's simply a matter of cleansing any residue and airing out the house of our soul!

This stage should actually invoke a wonderful feeling of self-satisfaction. Consider all the work we've gone through as we've sorted through the maze of belongings—and the corresponding inner work—to be able to see our current reality clearly. We can only do thorough "spring" cleaning when everything is put away and our house is in order. It's now time to scrub, vacuum, wash and polish to showcase our personal space to its full potential.

During this task we engage both the subconscious and conscious minds, as well as our physical body through each action. It's a functional, productive exercise, as we literally clean our homes through this intentional, meditative act of washing away the unwanted energetic remnants of our past.

One of the most unrelenting emotions to erase and be cleansed of is guilt. Guilt is a pure suggestion of the subconscious mind; however, hidden triggers allow unnecessary and misplaced feelings of guilt to surface frequently in our lives.

Some of these triggers are instilled in early childhood by the culture and society we live in and have no connection to inner guidance. We are made to feel guilty about little things any time we don't follow the current beliefs of others in our environment. The impact of being judged and found guilty of rather innocent actions, especially as a child, can be devastating. We must remember that those who instilled these erroneous feelings of shame and guilt were doing the same as was done to them. Again, in most instances we are *victims of victims*.

As children, we are taught to feel guilty about everything, often because something "appears" inappropriate to others. If we continue as adults to be concerned with the opinion of others, we set ourselves up for feelings of failure and guilt.

It is my opinion that organized religious teachings, as well as the institutions they have influenced, have led to the vast majority of guilt experienced on this planet.

One such example is that in the Catholic faith we are generally taught it is best to confess our perceived sins to a middle-man instead of delivering them directly to God. If we do not show the proper reverence to the priests—and what is proper varies from congregation to congregation, in my experience—we are labeled as sinners and deemed immoral.

This rejection and judgment cause an overall feeling of "badness" that we subconsciously retain. If we are repeatedly not pious enough or do not live our lives based on the moral judgment of others, we are considered a lost cause. Even if we succeed in eventually dismissing the labeling and judgment as the product of closed minds, we still feel disconnected and isolated.

Those in positions of power often use guilt to control others' behavior. At its core guilt is a natural instinctive guidance system to help us discern right from wrong, but this has been manipulated and corrupted throughout time, with the intention of controlling others usually for selfish reasons.

As a result of our learned guilt trigger, we feel our actions need to be punished; our heart doesn't say this, other humans do. Because we have become so detached from our inner voice and intuition, we end up following the voice—and judgments—of those around us. We therefore feel we are unworthy and deserve punishment, and continue to create a cycle of situations which cause us to experience more guilt. This is especially true of those with addiction issues.

We have an innate need to be punished, and if we don't feel that we have paid the dues of our actions, we repeatedly ask our conscious mind to find ways to ensure our failure.

In order to avoid perpetuating a feeling of guilt, moderate "earthly" punishment right after the fact—before the feeling of guilt has the time to set in—can be extraordinarily beneficial.

An example of this concept is found in some Native American traditions. When someone has done something considered morally wrong, the individual is sent to a cave where they remain alone for one month, eating only unsalted foods. They believe that if the act is appropriately punished, the subconscious mind knows inner justice has been served and things are shifted back into balance. Because of this, the individual will not sow the seeds of guilt, with concomitant new triggers and a cycle of re-enacting the same behavior.

It is noted that the punishment itself must be fair and aimed at soul redemption, rather than used as a tool for creating more damage. Once it is properly applied, it creates a sense that things have been dealt with and they can be allowed to wash away.

Misplaced guilt can gradually spread into all aspects of our lives, like weeds overtaking a lawn, resulting in destructive choices.

It is helpful to distinguish the difference between guilt and remorse. Guilt is what one feels if they have done something intentionally "wrong"; again, this is a very subjective matter, as some acts can be legitimately wrong or simply erroneously perceived, by ourselves and others. Regardless, guilt is the emotional response to having done—or thought— something about which we are ashamed.

Remorse is quite different. Remorse is triggered when we are genuinely sorry for an inadvertent action or when we have neglected someone or something. There was no intent to harm, and we feel genuinely sorry for what has occurred.

Chances are we feel guilty when instead remorse is a more appropriate response.

Guilt is a trap which keeps us focused on the past, reliving what we did wrong. Remorse is a much healthier, productive emotional response: acknowledge what occurred, take responsibility if appropriate, and then work toward not repeating the same incident. It is proactive and allows us to move forward whereas guilt produces stagnation.

Many prayers, and especially biblical psalms, are used to ease the guilt we feel and can be instrumental in understanding the mechanics of the conscious and subconscious minds. All we have to do is read between the lines and open our hearts to the truth hidden in the words. I say hidden truths, because they have been interpreted countless ways through the centuries. I suggest that we tap into our intuition as we read any sacred works (for that matter, when we read anything of importance); allow the truths to be absorbed not by the mind but by the heart, the seat of our soul.

As Jesus himself stated, according to Matthew 6:6 (King James), "But thou, when thou prayest, enter into thy closet, and when thou hast shut thy door, pray to thy Father which is in secret; and thy Father which seeth in secret shall reward thee openly." This passage says the true believer may pray to God directly, with no need to show or prove that he prays to fellow believers.

God can be reached simply by opening our hearts and listening within, with no need of an agent to speak on our behalf. God is always inside of us. God *is* us, and we can connect to the Eternal Mind by connecting with other living creatures and life forms, as the same energy of God lives within them.

We can begin our quest to understand the truth by simply substituting key words in prayers and sacred texts: God is the subconscious mind, the devil is our conscious mind; the enemies are the triggers; and sins are acts that we consciously accept even if our hearts do not believe we have sinned, causing us to feel guilty.

It is my belief that the wrath of God is nothing more than the punishment society or we ourselves insist upon when "sins" are deemed to have been committed. Certainly there are heinous crimes requiring punishment in order to keep the other members of a community safe; yet most guilt is on a much lower level not involving legal action. It is more personal, yet equally destructive. We subconsciously manifest what we have been convinced is the wrath of God when we feel profoundly guilty.

I am certain many will be outraged by my viewpoints, but I can only humbly set forth my observations and allow each person to find their own truth.

My most sincere hope is that by expanding our horizons and being open to new ways of perceiving age-old beliefs, we can open the door to true understanding and healing.

Once we allow our minds to be cleansed from the guilt that no longer serves a purpose, we will be able to truly clean house and finally invite fresh air to sweep through.

Take a deep breath and allow the air to flow and cleanse any negative influence of religion, society, caregivers, schools, etc. from your life, taking with it any lingering cobwebs of guilt and regret.

As with most tasks intended to repair or heal years of neglect, patience and perseverance are required. Please remember that some things cannot be scrubbed clean the first time; certain painful attachments and emotional triggers such as insidious, misplaced guilt are difficult to completely erase. Like stains on carpet and other stubborn residua, removing them will require commitment and elbow grease.

The longer we live side by side with misery, we learn to identify with it...it becomes our constant companion and we unknowingly merge with it. It stands to reason that throughout our lives, even after we've gone through this inner healing, there may be times when we find an emotional trigger has once again taken hold. We must not get frustrated. Instead, simply acknowledge it, release it, and cleanse the painful emotion away.

We should also keep in mind that any time we are attempting a new way of doing things, it requires repetition. Within these pages new tools have been introduced, and one must learn to work with them and do so repeatedly until it becomes habit. Teachers of yoga and other Eastern spiritual practices recommend persisting with a new program for forty days, because that is the amount of time necessary to trigger an inner shift.

But what if there are some burdens too deep to completely erase?

While it is usually best to remove negative remnants of painful experiences from our minds in order to break harmful patterns, sometimes the scars are simply too deep, too embedded. What we can do is view them as scratches and deep grooves cut into beautiful wooden flooring. We can't erase all blemishes and scarring, but we can clean and polish the wooden floor to its own perfection. The flaws, which are certainly in the eye of the beholder, add character and a more profound beauty to the foundation.

Cleansing isn't a one-time event. We must repeat these chores periodically to maintain cleanliness and wholeness. Just as negative thinking and self-sabotaging behavior became second nature over time, we must work with these new approaches to life until they merge with our every breath.

The final, most important thought to return to is forgiveness.

Because we incorporate so many feelings of guilt and feelings of being "less than" as we are bombarded by judgments imposed upon us—and we, mistakenly, allow it—it is *absolutely essential* we learn to forgive others and forgive ourselves.

When at any point you feel you haven't succeeded in walking through the steps to create a more authentic, whole life, forgive yourself! We are, after all, only human. We can always strive to do better, each step of the way, as we work toward being the most perfect us we can be.

In order to do this we must take the time to go within...go to that quiet internal space you created earlier and genuinely forgive yourself for what you perceive as failings.

As you wash dishes, stand in the shower or soak in the bathtub—any daily activity involving the healing power of water—"see" the water washing away these emotional obstacles. Basic rituals such as this are very effective in the cleansing process. See yourself being washed clean each day, washing away the layers of debris holding the beautiful essence of you from brilliantly shining through.

Chapter 8: Affirmations
As I clean my physical abode, so I cleanse the home of my soul

- I am the victim of victims, therefore I release guilt connected to past actions with which I no longer resonate.
- By dealing accordingly with experiences as they arise, I am now able to avoid storing unnecessary guilt connected to mistakes.
- I will deal with the residua of past blocks as I become aware of their lingering presence.
- I forgive.

Chapter 8: A Taste of the Spiritual Unknown
Since ancient times, water has been a symbol of purity and healing. Because of its fluid, feminine qualities, water is seen as the major tool in removing old patterns and in facilitating the process of rebirth.

In the Bible we are told that John the Baptist used water to purify the people who wanted to be reborn in Christ, and this practice is still heavily threaded through the many branches of the Christian faith.

Water is also used freely by other traditions to induce healing.

In the Italian Strega tradition, water is used to release spells aimed at healing, with disease washed away and the sick person instantly liberated by whatever was afflicting them.

On a very personal note, it is my family's belief that I am here on this Earth as a testament to the fact that such a practice works very well. When my mother was pregnant, she thought that she was having twins. The doctor tried several times to listen for two separate heartbeats, but only one was ever heard. One morning, while my father was away taking care of his dying mother, my mother went into very premature labor. When she arrived at the hospital she was taken directly to the delivery room and given a powerful pain reliever.

It was common practice at that time to anesthetize the mother. Through the haze of her narcotic-induced limited perception and in the midst of giving birth, my mother heard someone say very clearly, "The baby is dead."

Not long after this initial devastating announcement, much to everyone's surprise her labor pains started again. Shortly, another baby came into the world, this one still alive.

From the moment I was born prematurely at less than seven months' gestation, it was apparent that my own health was seriously compromised; my lungs were closed, I had a gastric infection, and I was extremely tiny and unresponsive to medical treatment. The doctors gave my parents little hope and after a few days waited for me to die.

Because of her spiritual beliefs, my mother sought the help of an acquaintance of my grandmother, an old woman known to work powerful healing spells.

The old woman told my mother she needed a personal object of mine, so she was provided with a booty I had worn in the incubator. She worked on it that same evening and gave it back to my mother who, following instructions carefully, threw it in the Arno River. The booty held my energy and the river the healing powers. My mother held the love.

The next morning I began to respond to treatment almost immediately and started to gain weight. Needless to say, the doctors were stunned.

In Voodoo, water is represented as two different faces: Yemoja, the mother of the ocean waters and the patroness of fertility, and Oshun, the gentle and sweet water of streams, lakes and rivers. Oshun is considered to be the sister of Yemoja, but her primary purpose is that of healing the heart and allowing people to know true love.

Oshun is represented by the color yellow and is associated with the solar plexus, the chakra which allows the storage of emotions and the release of instinctual impulses.

The gifts customarily presented to her are feminine in nature: jewelry, yellow vegetables and fruits, mirrors that she can use to see her own beautiful reflection, champagne, and yellow flowers. Another gift that Oshun loves is honey, but it must be tasted before being offered; legend teaches that, when alive, Oshun was a slave who was killed with poison-laced honey.

When seeking Oshun's intervention in creating a calm space, the practitioner may sit by the edge of a river, a lake or a stream. The gifts are to be placed directly on the river bank, after knocking on the ground three times, and then ask for help in finding peace within our chaos.

Chapter 9

The Kitchen
Recipes for Disaster, Remedies for Prevention

If you are to be, you must begin by assuming responsibility. You alone are responsible for every moment of your life, for every one of your acts.
Antoine de Saint-Exupery (author, "The Little Prince")

If your house is like mine, very few rooms are consistently dismantled as much as the kitchen. In the average home, the kitchen is the drop-off point, where everything gets dumped upon our return. Unless we're extraordinarily organized, this is where the mail, homework, toys, projects, and so much more collect.

No matter how often I try to keep it tidy, there is always something cluttering the counters. Even worse, there are always things on the floor creating a potential hazard.

I have stressed many times to all family members not to leave anything on the floor, especially near entryways where it is so easy to trip. Equally maddening are the puddles constantly found on the floor: drinks spill, mud and debris are tracked in, and ice cubes inevitably escape on their way from the icemaker into the glass, just waiting for someone to slip and fall.

Aside from the above dangers, this debris field is an invitation for a variety of pests to make their home in the kitchen. It drives me crazy, as it's all so preventable. Of course, I have repeatedly warned everyone about the dangers of such carelessness, but my words seem to disperse in the breeze that blows gently from the small kitchen window.

On Monday morning, after two days of what seems like a coordinated full-frontal assault on this one room, walking into my kitchen is a peril at best: the floor is alternately sticky and slippery, with shoes, toys, crayons, and bizarre items never seen before appearing in the most unexpected places. I can only stare speechless at the disaster before me.

Several years ago I sat down with my cup of coffee at my tidy little corner of the kitchen table and reflected on it all. As I tried to assess the damage and understand why such an avoidable mess keeps manifesting, I realized the kitchen reminded me of the path of life.

Although we try to make our journey as smooth as possible, there are always sticky and slippery spots around every corner. Since we are most always absorbed in multiple tasks, sometimes we can't see the spots and end up getting stuck or falling altogether; at other times we are fully aware of the existing spots but continue our reckless run, crossing our fingers and hoping for the best.

It's most frustrating when we trip over the very same obstacles we put in place ourselves. We rarely admit to this, as evidenced by my children swearing up and down, week after week, that they have no idea how the mess continues to appear. Yet, lo and behold, they inevitably stumble over something— usually the very items they left in the way—and they are shocked!

Most of us are no different, however. We all set our own obstacles and then act surprised when we run into them.

During a conversation about teenagers, my sister joked that parents spend half their daily energy trying to prevent their child's self-destruction. We laughed about this made-up statistic, but I quickly saw the truth in the statement. I began wondering why humans seem to spend so much time and energy sabotaging their lives.

When we pay attention, it doesn't take long to see there are countless examples of this type of self-destructive behavior.

We have become so conditioned to violence that we now *expect* to see only tragedy lurking behind every corner. We can watch ten inspiring, positive news segments and two negative ones, but at the end of the newscast we are likely to only remember the negative stories. Humans thrive on tragedy and drama, and the more drama they witness and experience, the more they feel connected with the rest of humanity.

I seldom hear anyone discuss an inspirational story at length, but it is extremely common to witness group discussions focused on a tragedy that has disseminated fear, pain, anger, and loss. Everyone wants to add their two cents and often blurt out very judgmental comments merely for the sake of attracting attention and validating their own fear or anger.

Granted, the negative stories are what the media presents, disproportionate to any good news stories. I'd like to think that if just as many inspirational stories were being broadcast, people would be focused on discussing them just as passionately.

While dispensing unfounded judgments and harsh comments toward others has become far too commonplace, we still tend to reserve the harshest judgments and treatment for ourselves.

We doubt our intuition; we undermine our thought processes and ability to respond to situations; and, most of all, we relentlessly criticize ourselves every step of the way. Even those who appear confident and self-assured on the surface need to feel that others approve of them and their actions; when they don't receive the desired approval, their fragile sense of security is gradually corroded.

I was introduced to Andrew a few years ago, a gentleman who seemed to have it all: a beautiful wife, three charming daughters, and a six-figure job executed from the comfort of his posh home. He led an absolutely golden life, at least on the surface.

Not long after meeting him, I discovered that his wife had recently asked for a divorce and that he was drinking heavily. Everything this man had built over twenty years crumbled in a few short weeks. He lost his job and his family moved out. Following close behind was a nasty divorce played out in the court system.

When I learned what had occurred in the interim since having met him, I felt his reaction was not only understandable but predictable. The rug had been pulled from under his feet so harshly that when he fell he didn't even know the direction he was facing.

He needed time to regroup and get back on his feet.

Family and friends worked overtime to help him through this crisis, but Andrew could not shake himself out of it. Pain and failure became his new identity. His drinking increased, as did his erratic behavior, leading him into deeper problems. He became negligent of his children and didn't pay his debts. His attitude toward life became cynical and his behavior unacceptable by societal standards.

No one within his circle of friends could understand how a man so in control and successful could fall so fast and not even attempt to get up.

If we take a closer look at Andrew's life, we can pinpoint several warning signs that help us better understand his tragic fall.

Raised in a stern, conservative Christian home, he felt out of place since early childhood. As a teenager, he secretly experimented with drugs and alcohol. No one in his family knew this, as he consistently presented a very well-behaved, clean-cut image to those around him.

As he got older, Andrew retained the two personas. In front of the world he was an exceedingly successful and God-fearing man, devoted to his family and the many responsibilities his lavish lifestyle imposed on him. Behind the curtain he continued to indulge his secret affair with alcohol and repress his feelings of inadequacy. He led two separate lives.

I recall thinking how very difficult that must be, and then realized many of us do the same thing, though to a less obvious degree.

After getting to know him better, I learned that although he was active in church and tithed generously, he felt no true sense of belonging. He didn't feel a connection with anyone and instead had created an outward image which imprisoned him. As we previously saw in the case of the always-bragging Angel, Andrew also did not miss a chance to boast about his affluence and accomplishments to anyone who would listen. It's fairly easy to see that many people who behave in this manner are filled inside with feelings of inadequacy.

For a surprisingly long time Andrew prevented his addiction from getting out of hand by burying himself in his work, but no one can live two separate lives forever. Some individuals crack sooner than others, but eventually the effort required to hide one's true identity cannot be sustained. When the crack splits wide open, the descent into hell is surprisingly fast.

Once everything was lost, Andrew felt as if he had nothing further to lose and thus indulged his demons around the clock.

I was curious as to what had led to Andrew's creation of two different personas all those years ago. After several sessions, I learned that in childhood Andrew had always felt different. He felt more adventurous and ambitious than his brothers and sisters, and longed to explore life in a different way than the one set forth in the blueprint of his family. Although he did not share the same religious beliefs of his parents, throughout his childhood he was completely indoctrinated in their rigid Christian principals. He acted as though he believed in order to maintain peace within the household; he had no doubt his father would have tossed him out onto the street had he known the truth. Those ideals were part of Andrew, even if he could not come to accept them in his heart.

The fact that he was doing something wrong by not believing was so deeply embedded in his consciousness that he felt guilty for being different, and especially for hiding that he was different. He was the outcast, the only member of the family who didn't fully embrace the idea of a savior and redemption of the soul.

To make up for this misplaced guilt, he took it upon himself to try to impress his family and others. This continued into adulthood when he focused on being a benefactor to the church. He may not have believed, but by doing this he would gain his parents' admiration. He married a girl with the same religious beliefs as his family, probably another action to win the approval of his parents. He immersed himself head first in creating a picture-perfect family, one that his parents would have been proud of.

Andrew and his wife never truly connected; they were merely partners who shared children and finances. More than anything, his wife was the picture of piety, the perfect mate to uphold the image he was determined to maintain.

When Anne became tired of competing with the other persona hidden behind her husband's charming exterior, the whole charade disintegrated.

The crushing weight of the loss brought him to his knees. Andrew had no marriage, no respect from his family, and most certainly had no sense of self. His golden image no longer intact, Andrew had nothing to lose, so he disappeared into the bottle and slipped even deeper into the abyss of despair.

Interestingly, in his heart he was relieved, as he felt this was the punishment he deserved for not fitting in with his family. He clung to the image of drunken recklessness, the most efficient tool to continue punishing himself.

In the past several years I have met many Andrews. Maybe their fall was not as hard, but the common denominator was always the same: guilt.

This is why it is so important to cleanse guilt from our hearts and minds, especially any guilt stemming from childhood experiences. It is corrosive and can lead to self-defeat. It causes us to intentionally place obstacles in our own path so that we will fall, proving to ourselves and others we were never worthy to begin with.

Many times as we try to fight our inner demons we end up hurting others in the process. The knowledge that we are hurting others makes us feel even guiltier, and more prone to seek further punishment.

Lives impacted by addiction are the perfect example of this. Family and friends are often crushed, fearing for their loved one and deeply affected by the addictive behavior. The addict, filled with sadness and remorse, repeatedly tries to resist the urges and overcome the addiction. Unfortunately, as hard as he tries, he slips and uses again, devastated that he has once more failed his loved ones. He doesn't really care that he has failed himself; nothing outweighs the desire for the drug or action to which he is addicted. Being painfully aware that his behavior hurts everyone around him leads to a new bout of guilt for which he needs to punish himself. It is a sinister cycle which leaves ravaged lives in its wake.

Ironically, it is often the support of others, and the simple fact that someone believes in him, which triggers another episode.

Any time he takes small steps away from addictive behavior, be it through rehabilitation or other means, he feels he is losing a grip on his own misery. He believes he is a terrible person, not deserving of their love and trust, and he believes—he knows—that he will fail them again. So, he does. After failing there is guilt, and the cycle continues.

This pattern explains why addiction is very rarely cured on a long-term basis *unless the decision to heal is initiated from a place of*

complete honesty and humility from the person who is addicted.
The inability to help a loved one battling addiction, until he is ready to commit to a path of wellness himself, can cause tremendous frustration and heartache. Indeed, it can lead to misplaced guilt on the part of the loved ones who are not able to "fix" the problem, with the inherent problems and struggles which accompany such feelings of helplessness.

There are no easy answers. DR. IHALEAKALA HEW LEN

A very interesting theory was introduced a few years ago by a psychologist who treated dangerous and socially-inept inmates. He was curious as to whether the behavior of the inmates could be changed, if only subtly, by changing *his* perception of *them*. He chose several inmates and each day dedicated a set amount of time to visualize them behaving in a way that was less violent and less self-destructive.

In addition to this, he would sit alone for a few minutes and repeat the mantra, "I love and I forgive." He did not direct those words to anyone else but himself. By healing inner blocks within his own mind, he was able to change the colors with which he Online: painted his world. Hawaiian process :"HO'OPONOPONO"

According to his report, even he was surprised when the inmates' behavior began to shift and they became much more responsive to his therapy. Although they were imprisoned for the most serious of crimes and therefore would never be free again, their lives behind bars measurably improved. They were able to interact with one another and with the correctional officers in a much more respectful way.

The following excerpts are from The Nature of Personal Reality, by Jane Roberts, which detail the principle behind the theory of the good doctor:

You cannot escape your own attitudes, for they will form the nature of what you see. Quite literally you see what you want to see; and you see your own thoughts and emotional attitudes materialized in physical form. If changes are to occur, they must be mental and psychic changes. These will be reflected in your environment. Negative, distrustful, fearful, or degrading attitudes toward anyone work against the self.

"...There are obviously ways in which you mold your own conditions, protect yourself from your own negative suggestions and those of others. You must learn to erase a negative thought or picture by replacing it with its opposite.

What you see in others is the materialization – the projection of what you think you are – not necessarily, however, of what you are. For example, if others seem deceitful to you, it is because you deceive yourself, and then project this outward upon others.

...True self-knowledge is indispensable for health or vitality. The recognition of the truth about the self simply means that you must first discover what you think about yourself, subconsciously.

People react to negative suggestions only when their own frame of mind is negative. Then we close ourselves off from the constructive energies we need.

You are a multidimensional personality, and within you lies all the knowledge about yourself, your challenges and problems that you will ever need to know. Others can help you in their own way... But my mission is to remind you of the incredible power within your own being, and to encourage you to recognize and use it." (Bantam, 1980)

In the past several years I have often suggested this same technique to those who have come to me for assistance. It is so very important to realize the necessity to forgive ourselves in order to release pain and blocks preventing us from moving forward to create the life we desire.

While about half the people I work with are consciously consumed with guilt, the other half are *subconsciously* consumed with guilt yet outwardly are not aware there is anything requiring their forgiveness. These are the people who tend to blame the world for all of their trials and tribulations. In the process of devoting so much time and energy blaming others for their misfortune, they are blinded to the obvious patterns manifesting in their world.

I advocate taking responsibility, not blame.

I understand some may find it hard to accept that we have responsibility in the unfolding of events, so I will offer a very simple, concrete way of viewing this.

Even if we are not ready to believe that thoughts contribute substantially to what we experience, it is easy to see that our behaviors trigger specific responses from the world around us.

Our behaviors and actions are in large part triggered by past experiences, so we often say certain things or act in such a fashion that prompts others to respond in a very predictable manner. Certain actions carry an energy which results in predictable responses from others and in our reality in general. Cause and effect.

The same is true of the energy of our thoughts, though it may take a little longer for the predictable response to manifest.

Until we take responsibility for our thought *pattern* (not individual, miscellaneous thoughts), as well as our actions, we shall perpetuate our own self-defeating cycle.

In this chapter we have examined self-destructive, self-sabotaging behaviors. Now let's take a look at possible remedies and preventive measures.

When our emotional damage is so severe that one requires assistance beyond the measures provided within these pages, I encourage professional therapy.

Our emotional health, emotional history, and emotional triggers are not to be taken lightly.

The focus of psychotherapy is that of bringing unresolved

issues to the surface. By discussing daily events, older blocks are gradually triggered and enticed into the open where they can be examined and assessed. This is very similar to what we achieved during the excavating and sorting of our conscious "closets" and subconscious "attic".

In therapy, results are rarely immediate, as the first thing that must happen is a process of building a path of trust between the counselor and the person being counseled.

Very often individuals abandon therapy before true results are achieved, basking in the personal illusion that they are already healed when even a few of the surface symptoms begin to ease. Sometimes they simply lose hope when, after months of talking, they still experience discomfort and disconnection from themselves or when, sadly, they can no longer afford the expense or time involved with professional therapy.

Dealing with intense emotions is one of our biggest challenges. Because of the society we live in, and the self-control imposed upon us since early childhood, the moment we feel intense emotions arise we quickly smother them, pushing them into the closet. As we have seen, however, the repressed emotions must be addressed at some point; if not, the energetic charge associated with these experiences mix with other unresolved feelings, creating a powerful weapon which ends up being used against us and others.

Bookmarking our emotions is a wonderful tool to be used during uncomfortable social events, times when expression of our true thoughts and feelings are deemed inappropriate. The emotional response triggered can be bookmarked—make a mental note to return to this—and dealt with later in a more comfortable, private setting. It is important to be sure to address the bookmarked feelings at a later time; by ignoring this very crucial step we would dishonor a commitment to ourselves. When we dismiss ourselves, we invite the same reaction from others.

Through the use of bookmarking our emotional floodgates are only dammed for a short while, allowing us the opportunity to deal with our feelings but also maintain our social integrity.

As mentioned previously, I am a proponent of meditation as a means of quieting one's mind in order to sort through emotional inner turmoil and work toward finding our true selves.

Most techniques on meditation are often misunderstood. I have heard the same excuse time after time: *I can't meditate.*

Everyone can meditate, just as everyone can breathe.

In the past few years, a great deal of literature has surfaced concerning this subject, most touting the beneficial effects of meditation on our emotional, mental, physical, and even spiritual well-being.

Unfortunately, people are often told that we have to achieve a state of complete mental silence when we meditate in order to receive any benefit. This is what discourages most people when they first attempt meditation. It is nearly impossible to shut out a busy world such as the one we live in and shift to complete silence and pure bliss at the snap of our fingers.

I will grant that, as in all disciplines, practice makes perfect; after allowing time to practice meditation, we can certainly open to an inner awareness which leads toward a more peaceful state of mind.

Remember how the term *meditation* is very similar to the word *mediation*? Slowly, and with patience, we can learn to quiet the mental chatter by allowing it to flow and not respond to the trivialities. Eventually, the chatter subsides and we hear another voice, a much more calm voice...a soothing voice which is there to guide us and be our best friend in this life.

This is the voice which has been trying to get through, telling us, "There's an obstacle ahead, pay attention!"

Years ago there was a popular phrase related to mental chatter: "Garbage in, garbage out." This is a very effective mantra or affirmation aimed at helping us recognize "garbage" thoughts and immediately send them to the trash bin. When we can recognize unnecessary, negative thoughts coming into our minds and learn to quickly dismiss them before they've had a chance to take hold, we can prevent mental clutter substantially, making way for our inner voice to be heard.

In conjunction with the "garbage in, garbage out" approach, another viable preventive measure, as well as a proactive creative tool, is to incorporate positive affirmations into daily life.

As we have previously seen, the subconscious mind will follow suggestions of the conscious mind. We can post positive affirmations on a message board in the kitchen or at our workplace; we can attach a sticky note to our bathroom mirror; we can hang a smiley face in front of our bed to greet us the moment we wake up; or we can listen to inspirational CDs and lectures.

Prayer is another immensely powerful tool we can work with daily. Through prayer, we open our heart to the Universe, ask for help, and then release the worries and attachments. Prayer and positive daily affirmations hold the power to reset our inner computer, so to speak, helping us create our lives from a more loving place.

We do not have to be religious in order to pray. Prayer can be seen as a way to give voice to what we long for in our hearts. After calling forth divine guidance, it is important to *believe* that things will somehow shift and then release the burden.

Rituals are a form of active prayer. Spiritual ceremonies and rituals have always played a central role in all traditions and cultures. Whether a ritual is performed as a solitary act, such as lighting a candle, or done with others, the underlying purpose is to connect with Spirit.

There are many positive steps we can take each day to not only work toward a state of healing and genuine happiness, but to simply enjoy these acts in and of themselves, with nothing expected beyond the joy of the moment.

Everything starts with a single act. As the first puddle I wipe from the kitchen floor is the initial act which eventually culminates in my entire house being clean, a single positive action can be the catalyst for life-altering attitudes and experiences.

Recognize when you are self-sabotaging and take steps to remove this pattern from your life; likewise, take steps to prevent the urge for self-sabotage from ever arising again.

With these empowering tools to help you maintain the structural integrity of the house of your soul, it is now time to give attention to honoring your unique beauty.

Chapter 9: Affirmations
I forgive who I was; I embrace who I have become

- As my clear perception grows, I am increasingly aware of the nature of the obstacles on my path.
- My self-destructive patterns are an indication of my inner triggers; I respect them and embrace the importance they have served in my life before I make a conscious choice to let them go.
- I release the guilt which I have erroneously associated with actions I could not help at the time.
- By healing the wounds deep inside of myself I have the power to change my reality.

Chapter 9: A Taste of the Spiritual Unknown
We all are aware of the numbing qualities of ice and the effect of extremely cold temperatures on humans and animals. When people and animals are exposed to freezing temperatures, the metabolism and ability to move are significantly slowed.

Because traditional magickal practice works on the assumption that everything is connected, we can slow down or stop a situation altogether, preventing further harm, by simply freezing an object that is sympathetically linked to the event.

The magickal practice of freezing unwanted situations is common throughout different traditions and is executed in a very simple manner.

Before going into the mechanics of it, it is important to acknowledge the fact that something frozen will not die; it will merely be incapacitated and unable to harm but still existing and able to be resurrected from its icy dimension.

In the case of self-destructive behaviors, including addictions, the ultimate way of truly eradicating the behavior is to go back to the source of discomfort and allow it to come to the surface where it will quickly dissipate. Blocking the symptom of a disease does not kill the disease; it relieves us from the pain for a period of time, during which hopefully we can work toward healing the root cause and think more clearly. The source of disease can be kept at bay until we are strong enough to deal with it and erase it, once and for all.

That said, let's explore the simple steps to freezing an unwanted situation as they are used by the European wise men and women.

All we need is a small piece of brown paper (such as a piece from a brown paper lunch bag), a lead pencil, a small cup or container, a small black candle, a little olive oil and salt, and, if possible, a little something belonging to the treated person.

Customarily, this kind of work is preferably done during the waning phase of the moon, when the celestial body is in its decreasing state.

Take the candle and anoint it with the olive oil while thinking about the thing you wish to stop. The anointing in this case should be executed by rubbing the oil on the body of the candle starting from the bottom and going up toward the wick, with the top of the candle point away from you. The idea behind this is that you are rubbing the unwanted situation away from you. Once the candle is properly anointed, sprinkle a little salt on it and set it in the candle holder. Light the candle. Write on the piece of paper what you want to be removed, then fold it away from you three times and place it inside the small container. It is important that the only thing written on the small piece of paper is exactly the situation you are trying to remove.

For example, perhaps you are trying to stop Uncle John from drinking too much. What you would write on the paper is: *Uncle John's drinking addiction and the damage his drinking causes him.* Nothing more. If you write, for example, *I would like to stop Uncle John*, then what you will freeze is your will to stop him.

Fill the small container with water and place it into the freezer; if you have a little something that belongs to the person, put that inside the container as well. The remains of the wax from the candle should be thrown into running water. As the water around the small paper freezes, the situation will stop. It may take a few days to get the situation out of your conscious mind so that it can be delivered to the subconscious for manifestation.

Do not despair, be patient.

This simple method can be used for the removal of any unwanted situation or behavior.

Chapter 10

Paint and Mirrors
Changing the Perception of Our Selves

We are the mirror, as well as the face in it.
Rumi

From our clean slate, we can now design a home which reflects our individual idea of beauty. The most logical place to start is by choosing our color scheme.

When choosing a color for our home's exterior, we often have conflicting thoughts. We long to use a bold color we adore but are concerned how others may perceive it. We might choose to "color within the lines" and go with a more acceptable color out of consideration for the neighbors and for the sake of conformity.

Choosing paint colors for our home is similar to choosing our wardrobe. While we should be encouraged to select colors which express our unique personality and make us most comfortable, sometimes we balance that with keeping other people in mind.

For example, a woman may genuinely love a particular blouse because of the color and style, yet she is aware that others find it extremely provocative and do not feel it appropriate to wear in public. This woman normally would not care what others think; however, she now has a teenage daughter. Out of respect for her child she chooses to not wear the blouse, as she does not want her own rebellious streak to possibly impact her daughter negatively in any way.

As with most things in life, moderation and balance are often required.

Our outer image is our ticket to connecting to the rest of the world. The impression others form of us will determine whether we shall have the opportunity to share the most special part of us which lies within. Some people can look past the exterior and be eager to learn more about a person; others are locked into that first impression. It is up to us how we choose to work with these very human variables.

We can always present ourselves exactly as we choose, not being concerned with how we're perceived, trusting those we want in our lives won't be hindered by appearances. Some may choose a moderate approach, wanting the opportunity to show people what they have to offer and not risk turning anyone off by potential misperceptions.

I've found that how we choose to present ourselves to the world can change frequently, especially as we go through various stages. Sometimes we're rebellious and focused only on what makes us feel good in the moment; at other times we are concerned, for perhaps practical reasons (job interviews, for example), about the way we are perceived by others.

Where we can express ourselves with abandon is on the inside of our home. The interior walls are crying out for us to bring them to life. These areas are our personal space. We can choose to do anything we'd like and express ourselves without restraint.

Once again, the concept of color applies to our lives on many levels.

As with clothes, some people limit themselves to painting with only neutral colors because that's what they grew up surrounded by. It's familiar, it's safe, it's acceptable. Others choose colors strictly based on what is in style that particular season; the fashion world dictates to them. Still others choose colors which are inviting and put people at ease, even if they are not personally drawn to the color.

It is a free spirit indeed who chooses to paint their life with colors reflecting their personal joy and passion.

You can paint each room a different color – there are no rules! You can get creative with stencils, sponge painting, and so many other ways to decorate these canvases. Keep in mind that the colors you prefer may change through time; you are not locked in to a certain style or color. Remember that throwing on a fresh coat of paint is the easiest way to surround yourself with an expression of your authentic self.

I encourage you to embrace your individuality and claim your personal sanctuary.

Throughout this book we have seen examples of people putting forth great effort to be accepted by others, sometimes taking drastic measures to create an image which cannot be maintained because it is not real.

In most cases we don't have to go through such Herculean attempts to be accepted and loved. I always find it intriguing that the image others see, versus how we see ourselves, is often very different.

This discrepancy of perception can be subtle or dramatic but is almost always correlated with our inner image.

A few years ago, a dear friend presented me with a Yule gift in the form of a beautiful, handmade mirror to hang in a place of prominence.

Taken aback by the originality of the present, I asked if there was any special place I should hang the mirror. Her response was, "It should be in a place where you can see it often. Remember that a mirror can be your best friend."

Although she had spoken those words casually, the message behind them kept me up for several hours that night.

Is a mirror truly our best friend?

In my personal experience I was never particularly fond of staring into mirrors, not because I hated my image but because mirrors are the unfortunate messengers of any flaws. As humans, we are intimately connected to our reflection and can feel undermined by flaws.

No matter how attractive someone is considered by society's standards, they may feel their reflection is unattractive. I recall hearing Pamela Anderson being interviewed about the problems within her marriage at the time, saying she accepted his abuse because she felt it was deserved because she was too ugly and stupid.

The majority of people see her as one of the most attractive women in the world. However, she saw something completely different when she stared at her own image in the mirror.

It is frightening to see this same type of split perception manifesting in the dramas unfolding for our youth. This is why it's vitally important we all speak up for true beauty and wisdom and not consciously promote the media's agenda of focusing on shallow, even unhealthy, images.

Some of the most heartbreaking examples come from the many cases of eating disorders and body image disorders afflicting our children. I know one such young girl and her family. Fortunately, this young girl was able to battle the inner demons that led to this distorted image of herself, one vastly different from what the rest of the world saw, yet it is a daily struggle.

According to her father, this young girl was subtly influenced by the bombardment of media and societal messages aimed at promoting a leaner, "skinnier" image. Because of their joint ordeal, and the understanding that their words can bring healing and hope to others, father and daughter travel extensively, speaking at schools assemblies and other functions. The father has even written a heart-wrenching book about their experience and is hoping that his agonizing journal of fear and perseverance will bring a tiny light to illuminate the journey of many still struggling through the same dark tunnel.

Aside from body image distortions, we can also have erroneous perceptions of our inner selves. We can view ourselves as "bad" and "ugly", while others are attracted to the good aspects of our character that we choose not to see.

So often it is all about where our focus lies. Our perceptions and perspectives.

I have often wondered if we see exactly what others see and vice versa. How do we know?

The most scientific means of studying perception of which I am aware is the Rorschach inkblot test. The inkblot test is actually a method of psychological evaluation, not perception per se. Psychologists use this test to try to examine the personality characteristics and emotional functioning of their patients.

While the validity of the science behind how people interpret these inkblot images is under scrutiny, one aspect is not disputed: *People do see different things when viewing the exact same image.*

A person's past experiences and programmed behavior, as well as response to various stimuli, can certainly play a role in how one responds to such a test. From a spiritual standpoint and a school of thought within quantum physics, everything is light; it is our own perception that gives the light a certain shape and color. It is therefore safe to assume that each person creates an image of the light by using the blueprints stored in their own subconscious. If those blueprints are faulty in the original design, the image that is created is erroneous as well.

Looking within ourselves is similar to looking in a mirror. If we pay attention to the mirror itself, it is very hard to achieve 100% flawlessness. No matter how many times we go over it, there are always a few streaks that escape our attempts at perfection.

If we can imagine seeing our inner reflection through a hazy, foggy mirrored surface, our image would be unclear and distorted. With some elbow grease and the right agent we can clean it so that the reflection isn't completely distorted, but it is probably wise to accept the truth that there is no such thing as a perfect mirror, and therefore no such thing as a perfect image.

There will always be slight distortion.

The way we perceive ourselves is nothing more than the reflection of our own inner state. As within, so without. As our subconscious blocks become more accessible and ready to be removed, the flaws in our mental mirror will become less noticeable.

Rather than accepting the twisted image concocted by our bruised ego, we will finally begin to see ourselves for who we truly are: beautiful, timeless, and boundless human beings.

As you hang mirrors in your freshly cleaned and painted home, consider one of the three tenets of the use of mirrors within feng shui: reflection. It is said that when you place a mirror in your home, you must pay attention to what is being reflected in it. In feng shui terms, the mirror is doubling that energy by creating a virtual duplicate within the space of the reflection. For example, if your mirror is reflecting a pile of clutter and unpaid bills, the reflection is a symbolic doubling of your untidiness and debt. On the other hand, if the mirror is reflecting a loving memento such as a family photo during a wonderful vacation, the mirror is symbolically doubling your family's happiness and enjoyment.

Hang the mirrors lovingly and gaze into them often, with gratitude and reverence.

Chapter 10: Affirmations

I smile at my reflection, for my true self is hidden behind my image in the mirror

- The way I present myself on the outside is a mirror image of my inner feelings about myself.
- I change the way I see my outer image, therefore my inner image grows more positive.
- I refrain from judging others by their outer appearance; rather, I will get to know their true self who lives within.

- Taking care of my body is the first step on the path toward caring for my soul.

Chapter 10: A Taste of the Spiritual Unknown

Throughout the world and especially embedded in European traditions, we find many spells for glamour.

Hoping to take the breath away from every person of the opposite sex who lays eyes on us, glamour spells have been heavily sought through the ages to improve our image to others.

As we continue to walk on our journey to self love, we will use one of the glamour spells to improve the way we appear to *ourselves*.

All we need is a good bottle of bath bubbles, a glass of champagne, perfume, fragrant candles of choice, a handful of pink or red rose petals, some sexy music, and the photo of a person we consider gorgeous.

After drawing a warm and sensuous bath full of bubbles, we sprinkle the rose petals in the tub and spray a good whiff of perfume. Music plays in the background as we get in the tub.

Living in the moment is very important right now. We must *feel* the sensuality of each instant and be aware of our bodily sensations.

The water gently caresses our naked skin and the fragrance of the perfume intoxicates our senses. The flower petals softly float over the mirror of the water, nudging us with their velvety touch every time we move.

All we feel is pleasure; all we hear is soothing, sensual music; all we see is beauty. We bask in those feelings for a few minutes, and then look at the photo we have chosen. We must look at the small details and record them in our minds.

After we have done so, we put the picture away and visualize the person photographed as if he or she were standing in front of us. We appreciate the beauty of their features and the light in their eyes.

We know that the inner light found within their gorgeous shell is the same light that lives inside of us, so we can fuse with them and merge with the beautiful image of their body.

In our mind's eye, we see them coming closer and closer to us, until we can smell their fragrance, feel the silky softness of their hair, and see the perfect luminosity of their complexion.

The image continues to come closer, and it slowly merges with us. We feel our own features morphing to accommodate the beautiful stranger.

Once the image is completely fused with us, we embrace the inner and outer beauty and look forward to going out into the world. We feel the gaze of men and women burning on us, as they stare in awe of our beauty. We see ourselves as beautiful, desired, and loved. We think of all the new opportunities we shall be able to enjoy, and the wonderful loves that will make their way into our lives.

Chapter 11

Flowers and Décor
Adding Beauty to Our World

Beauty is truth - truth, beauty - that is all ye know on earth, and
all ye need to know.
John Keats

Since ancient times, flowers have been a symbol of beauty. Our predecessors used them as offerings to Gods and Goddesses because of the breathtaking perfection of their colors and designs. In modern times, they are offered as gifts to symbolize our affection.

When it comes to decorating a home and adding beauty to our surroundings, flowers are an affordable item to add to our list. They are sold everywhere, from convenience stores to specialty florists, in a variety of price ranges. Even so, I find that one single daisy picked from my backyard by one of my children, placed lovingly in a Dixie cup, radiates a pure beauty throughout the home and to all who enter.

Humans crave beauty. It's as simple as that. Beauty is our connection to the Divine, from which many have become detached. It's a residual silver string that links us to the wonders of the Universe like an umbilical cord.

When we feel our world crashing around us, we become numb to the beauty that can be found each day. We read about it in works of literature and may spend afternoons browsing through art museums, but many feel beauty is a fleeting concept, reserved for the enjoyment of the fortunate few. For the rest of us, beauty has become something reserved for special occasions.

I have observed that when depression and apathy set in, beauty is almost disturbing to the senses; it feels intrusive, creating a stark contrast to the gray walls closing in. It's as though beauty taunts us, emphasizing our emptiness and despair.

We are bombarded by unrealistic images of beauty in magazines and on TV: models and actors airbrushed to physical perfection, luxury homes out of the reach of all but a few, and tropical resorts most of us will never have a chance to see.

It's easy to see how our self-image can take a beating with this deluge of shallow beauty, presented as the holy grail of modern life. We wonder why these beautiful things are shoved in our faces when we can't *be* them or experience them.

Some of us feel we don't deserve such wealth or luxury; some resent those who are living this media-created "beautiful" life, and walk around with a chip on their shoulder.

The beauty-and-riches game is also a study in the duality of contemporary life.

Most of us were taught to be content with the boundaries of our world and never be pretentious, yet we still love to watch the rich and famous. It's popular to voice our disgust with the media's fixation on celebrities in this Paris Hilton world, but there is a strikingly large audience for salacious stories involving those in the spotlight.

I recently read a startling article which reported that the day after 500,000 people had perished from a typhoon in Indonesia, primetime news shows in the United States were featuring the birth of a Hollywood celebrity's daughter.

The underlying question posed in the article was this: Have we become so shallow that one child born into wealth and fame takes priority over the story of thousands of children who lost their parents and everything they are familiar with, children who are starving to death?

Maybe we have. The scales of our value system have tipped

over beneath the weight of superficiality.

We have begun to live vicariously (and voyeuristically) through the joys and sorrows of the rich and famous. Meanwhile, our own worth has become insignificant and our ability to perceive genuine beauty has disappeared.

Beauty is has become equated with monetary value. We feel we can't witness a spectacularly brilliant sunset unless we are on an exotic Polynesian island or that we can't express romantic love without the offering of a flawless diamond.

In Western society a diamond is probably the most prestigious gem, one which people work countless hours toward purchasing. What is it about a diamond that makes it deemed more beautiful than other precious gems?

I have asked this question for years, with no adequate reply ever given. After observing our culture, I have come to the conclusion that the determining factor of worth is expense. The diamond is the most expensive of precious gems; therefore people see it as the most beautiful.

Again, the scales of perception are off kilter. If something does not risk sending us to the poorhouse when we purchase it, it loses its allure. In reality, the diamond is no more precious than all the other gems in the pantheon of jewels; we have simply anointed it as such because owning one makes *us* feel of more value.

True beauty has nothing in common with the media's version perpetually broadcast into our homes. The essence of beauty is in everything, surrounding us each and every day if we are willing to see it. It can come in surprising forms and from unexpected directions.

Consider the beauty of a snowflake. The following excerpt does just that, taken from the book, *Honey from Stone*, by Chet Raymo:

Has the mystery of the snowflake, then, been entirely plumbed? Certainly not! Physicists are content that they can

126

explain the hexagonal symmetry of the crystals, but they can say little about the delicacy of the branching and the extraordinary congruity of the six points. For these things, science has provided only the beginning of an understanding. It is clear that particles of airborne dust provide the nuclei about which snowflake crystals begin to grow. Without dust, there would be no snow.

...But the apparent stability of the ice crystal, like the apparent fixity of the mountain, is an illusion...faults in the crystal–places where there are extra hydrogen atoms or missing atoms–jump from place to place like unruly children in a teacher's classroom. And somehow, in the midst of this atomic caprice, the snowflake acquires and retains an ordered form. We are in the face of one of nature's most profound mysteries: how beauty and structure arise from a delicate balance of order and disorder.

...Physicists can only guess at how symmetry is maintained across the whole crystal as molecules of water attach themselves at random around the crystal's growing edge. Some physicists think that vibrations of the crystalline lattice are the instruments of communication, vibrations that are extremely sensitive to the shape of the crystal. If this is so, then the growing snowflake maintains its symmetry in the same way that members of an orchestra stay in consonance, by sharing the sound of an ensemble. The snowflake's beauty, then, is orchestral! The facultas formatrix is vibration. Nature shudders in its sublimity. Atoms dance to inaudible music. The cloud jams. The rock jives. The lake's still surface boogie-woogies." (Cowley Publications, 2005; Page 56)

This amazing book offers countless examples of how the true beauty of nature cannot be created in a lab or in a factory. True beauty has no monetary value. The snowflake is an example of a beautiful miracle available to all who encounter it, free of charge.

Once we see beauty in the world around us, we will know we have the resources to bring authentic beauty into our lives. True beauty is in the single daisy picked from the backyard or side of the road; the openhearted beauty of greeting a stranger; or the offering of our sandwich to a stray dog or cat. We can attract beauty by observing the staggering amount of perfection that is all around us.

Throughout our day we witness countless miracles, but we have forgotten how to see with our hearts. We no longer recognize the breathtaking perfection and beauty of the natural world and all life within it.

The old saying "stop and smell the roses" does not speak merely of living in the moment; it also wisely suggests we must see beauty in things that have no price tag.

The child who pours all of his love into crafting a gift for his mother may not produce a gift of store-bought quality, but it is a one-of-a-kind production by a perfect designer, infused with the light and passion borne of pure love and devotion.

Understanding this concept is fundamental to manifesting beauty in our world. When we look into the eyes of a vagrant, we should be able to see the light of the Universe, the perfection of design that is at the core of every being. Stopping short and avoiding eye contact due to someone's appearance would be the same as choosing a gift made in a factory over the heartfelt effort of a child.

As with every other stage of recreating the house of our soul, adding beauty to our world starts with simple steps. We can take a moment to observe a tree that has made it through a storm and rejoice in its example of endurance. We can watch our child play and be thankful. We can pick a wild flower on the side of the road and use it to beautify our home, giving it the same place of honor as an expensive heirloom rose; or, we can leave the flower alone and simply bask in its beauty, acknowledging it has a specific reason to be there, playing its own silent mesmerizing tune in the harmonics of nature.

Ultimately, the secret to beautifying our world is in realizing there is nothing to attract; beauty is always around us, willing to open the curtains to its majestic shows and provide the opportunity to savor the power of connecting with our true selves.

We must allow ourselves to see it and understand that we deserve to have beauty in our lives.

We are beauty.

Open the windows and allow light in. Let the scenery you are surrounded by be part of your home décor; choose to find the beauty around you.

Take a special gift or any item that has great meaning and display it in a place of prominence where you can see it each day. It matters not what others may think; this is your sanctuary, so envelope yourself in treasures that open your heart.

Cook a favorite dish, one which radiates a fragrant memory of love and joy throughout your home.

Turn off the television and turn on music that makes your heart sing!

Once we make a conscious choice to accept our connection to everything around us, we will then understand that we are an irreplaceable instrument in the universal orchestra. Without our unique melody, the masterpiece is incomplete. If we choose to see with our hearts and acknowledge that we belong to the Whole, the beauty of the Universe will unfold directly in front of our eyes in the form of sounds, images, fragrances, and moments of the heart, all to adorn the house of our soul.

Chapter 11: Affirmations

The illusion of beauty comes with a price; true beauty is free and bountiful

- Acceptance of beauty in my reality is one connection to higher realms.

- I perceive inner and outer beauty with my eyes and my heart.
- Beauty cannot be reproduced artificially, only the illusion.
- The house of my soul is perfect for me. The Universe makes no mistakes.

Chapter 11: A Taste of the Spiritual Unknown

In today's busy world it is sometimes hard to take the time to see the wondrous beauty displayed all around us.

When my first son was born, my husband, who previously seemed unaffected by the pregnancy, was in total awe at the sight of this tiny being making his grand entrance into the world.

Suddenly, he felt as though he could float off the ground. He went outside to get a breath of fresh air after having spent many long hours captive in the hospital room.

It was the heart of winter but John was unable to feel the cold; he only felt the total bliss which had seized his body and mind. He walked around and saw the world differently than he had only hours earlier.

To him, the sky had never been such a cobalt blue, the breeze had never been that soothing and uplifting, and the people walking around all seemed happy and able to share his joy.

That particular day, the sky had not been any special color, nor had the people walking by been overtaken by some strange virus that affected the pleasure center of the brain. The only thing that was different on the day of his first son's birth was the way John felt when he looked around.

We take for granted the beauty of our world and don't appreciate it unless it comes in an expensively presented package. The truth is, beauty is always there, waiting patiently to be noticed. We must be fully present and in the moment to absorb it completely.

In New Orleans a very popular way to get in the moment before working a spell or a "root" is to allow ourselves to truly see, hear, and feel what is around us. Once one can get into the present moment, consciousness shifts to the dimension of Spirit where time does not exist and where beauty is savored like a good meal, slowly and entirely.

The way it is accomplished is very straightforward:

We must sit still and say out loud the name of three things we see around us, then three things we hear, and finally three things we feel. Then we do that again in groups of two at a time, then one at a time. After that, we start again in groups of three, then two, then one, until we *feel* the beauty of everything that surrounds us.

It is a very simple exercise, but it's amazing how helpful it is in turning on the switch of our perception. Suddenly we are able to hear, see, and feel things to which we were previously oblivious. The white noise becomes a concert of different beautiful instruments, all harmoniously playing in perfect tune. For the first time we realize the perfect fusion of stimuli all around.

In a world full of fast-paced distractions, this exercise is a useful tool which will allow us to claim our own exquisite island of peace in the midst of chaos.

Chapter 12

Putting Out the Welcome Mat
Welcoming a New Life

As human beings, our greatness lies not so much in being able to
remake the world...as in being able to remake ourselves.
Mahatma Gandhi

The hardest work is now behind us. Only a few final touches remain before we can invite the rest of the world in to share the joy of our renovated home.

As we stand in the front yard, we appreciate the freshly-painted exterior, the sparkling new roof, and the flower garden providing a brilliant show, free of charge.

To passersby, this house radiates the love of those living within and makes them long to come inside. After a few days, the excited neighbors do just that. Trays of goodies in hand, they make their way to the front door, looking forward to meeting a new friend. They walk to the front porch and are ready to ring the bell when something unexpected catches their eye.

A faded old door mat stands out from the freshly painted exterior, with a still visible message which cools their enthusiasm. In spite of the home's inviting appearance, the message "Go Away!" takes them by surprise, and they look at one another in astonishment.

The message is clear. There is no need to ring the doorbell and introduce themselves; they are not welcome.

Inside, we watch as the neighbors walk away and make no attempt to stop them. We have mixed feelings about having visitors. We are ashamed and disappointed that we did not invite them in, but at the same time we are relieved they have gone. We want to keep our home as perfect as possible, without the potential for others to create a mess. Also, we are still in the habit of fearing unexpected company due to our embarrassment about the clutter and mess we used to live in. Our new reality has yet to fully sink in.

We aren't consciously aware that the old mat is still there, proclaiming its isolating message. We have been so engrossed in repairing and decorating that the mat merely became an invisible tool we used to avoid tracking in more dirt from the outside.

In life, this situation is more the rule than the exception. We go through a staggering amount of work to clean up our life and repair our flaws, but we still hold on to the barriers that have isolated us in the past.

Now that we feel renewed and refreshed, we are afraid contact with the outside world will spoil what we have created. It all feels very fragile. We want to share of ourselves, but we are afraid.

Anyone who has just finished cleaning their home is familiar with the mixed feeling we struggle with when a friend calls and says that she is on her way to see us—with her two toddlers. We are happy and proud to show our beautiful home, yet we know that once they are gone it will take even more work to reset the clock to how it looked before their arrival. We don't want to appear rude and do want to see them, so we reluctantly whisper, "Sure, come on over," praying for divine intervention to control the natural gift children have to create destruction and mayhem.

In the past I found myself almost stalking company around the house, cloth in hand, ready to wipe away any stain or crumb they may leave in their wake.

I have discovered, however, that all I have to do is clearly state that I have just cleaned house and tell the children to be sure to put things away after they are finished playing with them. I do not allow any food or drink to be taken into certain rooms.

Once my rules and expectations are stated clearly, things run smoothly and I can enjoy my guests. We often assume we will not be heard or that our requests will not be honored. I have found that most people are more than willing to comply with our wishes, as long as we find a way to clearly express them.

Learning how to express our boundaries and expectations is a necessary aspect to creating and maintaining our new lives with integrity. The other part of this equation is for us to realize that *the rest of the world is not out to hurt us in any way; we are the only ones harming ourselves by not clearly expressing the way we feel.*

Stating how we feel can be done respectfully and is very empowering. It is not meant to control others; it is simply a means to avoid unpleasant occurrences that will undeniably unfold if we don't take steps to prevent them.

By telling my children's friends that we can only eat in the kitchen, I am not being disrespectful to them; I am merely letting them know that I respect and love my home, and that they should do the same. After all, I would not dare go to their house and use a melting ice cream cone as a magic wand, twirling it over the living room carpet! It is up to me to clarify my expectations.

What I have discovered over the years is that most people are relieved to know what my boundaries are within my home. When we step onto someone else's territory, it is unsettling not to know what we should and shouldn't do.

There are people who will get offended if guests don't make themselves at home and grab something from the fridge themselves. There are others who are highly offended if we lay our coat over the loveseat in the entrance, though we had no idea this was "beloved Aunt Nancy's precious loveseat", for display only. How could we know?

Embarrassment and hurt feelings could have been avoided had the host simply stated that the delicate loveseat is there only for show.

Being around children is a wonderful way to learn this lesson. They thrive on set boundaries and are able to make conscious decisions based on the availability of choices in front of them.

Throughout our lives most of us try to please one another; the problem lies in the fact that we often don't know what is required to do so.

This pattern is most evident in couples, be they a new couple or partners who have been together for decades. Each partner *expects* the other to just *know.*

As romantic as mind reading may appear, this expectation is foolish and leads to unnecessary heartache and grief for both partners.

Until we have repeatedly done the work required to be in touch with our authentic desires, we are barely able to figure out what we want, let alone try to determine what another soul wants.

Each of us is different, and we all filter information based on the scale of our own perception, largely affected by our environment. A good example of this concept is offered through a family friend.

Jenny is married to a man who was born and raised in an entirely different culture. In his world, prior to moving to the United States certain holidays were not celebrated. Upon moving here, he was overwhelmed by an array of holidays, mostly commercially conceived.

Anyone who knows them can see he would walk into blazing flames for his wife and family, yet he seemed totally oblivious to his wife's disappointment when these holidays went unnoticed.

Rather than explaining that celebrating a particular holiday was important to her, she remained silent. She expressed her disappointment by getting angry over trivial things around the times of the missed holiday.

If she had voiced her desire to celebrate a particular holiday because it is something that is part of the culture she grew up in, her husband would have gladly indulged her, even if it was meaningless for him.

In yet another example provided by Jenny and Asim, we can see how stating our expectations and sharing our perspectives can wipe away rancor and misunderstandings.

Being raised in a world where necessities take priority over luxuries, Asim grew up with one dream: To have a stable life with financial security.

He focused on getting a good education which, unfortunately, came with sizeable debt. After finishing school, his goal was to pay off the loans and provide a stable financial foundation for his family to grow. For Asim, stability meant having a roof over his head and food on the table; it meant not having to worry about the necessities that he had to do without so frequently while growing up. He gladly worked diligently to provide for his family. In his mind he was the provider, which is how he expressed his love for his wife and family.

For Jenny, raised in a much more privileged world, this concept was impossible to accept. At twenty-five years of age she had spent the greater part of life being the focus of her parents' attention and devotion. As the youngest child, her parents never denied her anything and lavished her with material gifts throughout her life.

Once married and living away from her parents, reality hit. Money was tight, her home was not what she was accustomed to, and her husband was unavailable, spending most of his time at work. Although she understood his commitment to work, the time spent away from her felt like a personal affront and she began to fear he was willfully neglecting his family.

After endless hours of childrearing and running a household with very little money, she lost sight of everything and was unable to look at the bigger picture of future stability. Had Jenny sat down with her husband and expressed that she was touched by his efforts but needed more personal time as a couple, he would certainly have taken more notice. Instead, she left those words unspoken, simmering slowly in the pot of resentment.

Finally, after coming to terms with the fact that things were never going to change unless she did something, Jenny decided to write Asim a letter explaining how she felt. Understanding how she experienced life from her perspective enabled him to understand her needs. The same occurred when he voiced his side of things, and they were able to reach common ground about their daily lives as well as their future.

When we are clear within ourselves about our desires, expectations and boundaries, we can be more open to the expectations of others, creating a wonderful tapestry.

In my novel, *The Book of Obeah*, the wise Maman Marie attempts to teach this life lesson to Melody, a young woman in search of guidance. Maman Marie simply states, "True power is not in changing events from unfolding around us, but in changing the way those events affect our world."

Rather than keeping the doors and blinds closed and savoring our new sanctuary in isolation, wrapping ourselves in a tight cocoon so that others won't have a way to reach us and harm us, remaining open to life and all it has to offer will bring much more depth to our experience.

It is up to us to decide what is and isn't acceptable and then learn to express these decisions, still honoring the fact that others in our world have the same choice to either accept or reject our point of view.

It is also important to appreciate that we are now much stronger and resilient. The pain we allowed to be inflicted on us in the past has been identified and scrubbed clean. If it needs another cleaning to remove the residue, we must take time to do so and not let the past mar the potential for joy in our Now.

During the hard work of restoration undertaken throughout these pages, we have created a much sturdier structure that will withstand the harshness of the elements.

We need not fear meeting new people; we can rest assured that we now have the newfound ability to stand up for ourselves, with integrity. Once our perceptions and self-image have changed, we will find the people around us interact more respectfully, mirroring the respect we finally feel toward ourselves.

Welcoming others into our lives offers the potential for wonderful experiences we may have missed if we kept ourselves captive within the familiar interior walls.

There will most likely continue to be people who come into our experience to provide an opportunity for growth and under-standing, or to remind us who we truly are and what we most desire through unpleasant interactions. There will also be many souls who will join us on our new path, providing support and encouragement along the way.

By keeping the front door locked and the unwelcome mat in place, we deny others the potential to see our authentic beauty and gifts, and we deprive ourselves of a more expansive, more loving reality.

So, it's time to take a trip to the store to purchase a new mat, one which will confidently let all who come our way know that visitors *are* welcome.

Wake up each morning anticipating miracles, including those in the form of human angels who most certainly walk among us. Welcome them onto your path and into your life.

When the neighbors return, you know they will ring the doorbell this time; the message they are greeted with has now changed. They know they are welcome. Open the door widely and invite them in, displaying the results of your hard work.

Perhaps when the cookies and coffee are gone and the initial visit comes to a close you will have enjoyed one another's company so much that you will receive an invitation to their home. Now that you have opened your home and shared your inner sanctuary—now that you have genuinely connected—you can look forward to doing just that: Entering their sanctuary and getting a glimpse into the house of their soul.

Chapter 12: Affirmations
I establish new boundaries; I welcome others into my world

- I graciously allow others into my life.
- I see obstacles on my path and acknowledge their message.
- My power is in controlling the way events affect my reality, not in controlling the events themselves.
- As I connect with the world I connect with myself.

Chapter 12: A Taste of the Spiritual Unknown
Anytime doors and portals are mentioned, Elegba will always show up to claim his rightful place as the opener of doors.

This gentle yet powerful old spirit will always oblige our desire to open ourselves, and he will stand guard to make sure that we do so safely.

Throughout this book, we have approached the task of cleansing our soul by imagining our life as a home in need of repair and deep cleaning. We have gone from room to room, removed the trash, fixed the structures, swept the cobwebs and redecorated.

Now we need a special gift to ourselves, something to protect our home.

Who better to protect than the keeper of the doorways himself? By giving Elegba his own corner near the entrance of our home, we invite him in to help us guard the entryway to our soul.

In countries where the religion of Voodoo is widespread, a small statue of Elegba is commonly seen near the front door of the home or business. In front of the statue are offerings that are regularly replaced with new ones, usually on Mondays.

In my home, I don't only have one statue of Elegba near the door, I have two! In front of my statues I usually place a small plate of dried corn, a small bottle of liquor, and a cigar with matches. A corncob pipe is a favorite as well; Elegba likes tobacco, the fashion in which it is offered is in the heart of the person offering it.

Sometimes when I make fresh coffee in the morning, I also place a small cup on the little table that houses Elegba's makeshift home and imagine him smiling benevolently while he joins me. I find my house feels lighter and more pleasant when I bring Elegba gifts, so I expect that I will continue to do for many years to come.

For anyone who is interested in doing the same, a small statue can be purchased from one of the many websites that offer Voodoo products or can even be made by crafting a poppet. As explained in one of the previous chapters, buying or crafting the perfect symbol or offering is not what is important. What is important is the heartfelt intention to honor ourselves and others.

The offerings can be anything that the heart suggests. Elegba is not pretentious, and will be grateful for anything that is respectfully given with an open heart.

Chapter 13

Housewarming Party
An Attitude of Gratitude

The present moment is the only moment available to us, and it is the door to all moments.
Thich Nhat Hanh

Our home is finally in order, an honest reflection of who we are and what we desire in life.

We have cleared out the trash to make way for the new; we have removed much of the old and rebuilt with sturdy, reliable materials; and we have cleaned, painted, polished and decorated to our heart's content.

This process required that we learn to step outside of ourselves — or, more appropriately, step way *inside* of ourselves — to truthfully assess our own perceptions. By employing new tools and armed with a new perspective and a hefty dose of patience, we have turned what was a shell of a structure into an inviting, warm home.

Undeniably, we have succeeded in creating a beautiful, nurturing sanctuary.

We have learned to invite others in with an open heart and have shared of ourselves, and can now look forward to developing these relationships further.

The final item on our list seemed an impossible goal when we began this journey of discovery and healing. It's time to invite everyone we know to a party to celebrate our accomplishment.

Much to our amazement, we are completely at ease making phone calls and sending out invitations. We're not only at ease, we're growing more excited by the minute!

Suddenly, we're stopped in our tracks. What if people bring gifts? After all, they're being invited to celebrate our new home and it is still customary to bring housewarming gifts. We didn't consider this; our only intention was to share our joy, nothing more.

Panic and nervousness set in and we're tempted to call the whole thing off. The thought of people coming to see us, bringing gifts, expecting us to open them in front of everyone...it's too intimidating!

Rather than be excited at the possibility of receiving wonderful gifts for our new home, we're mortified.

Although receiving gifts and blessings should always be a pleasant experience, many resist the simple gesture of accepting anything, from anyone.

While visiting my husband at work several years ago, I suddenly sneezed. A gentleman sitting on one of the chairs in the waiting room heard me and uttered the usual, "God bless you." I thanked him rather absentmindedly.

His gaze never left me. "Yes, but do you accept it?"

It was a straightforward question, but I was stunned into silence. No one had ever asked me that, nor had I ever heard this question posed of anyone before.

I smiled, unable to say anything. So he repeated his question, firmly yet gently. "Do you accept it?"

Who was this stranger and what did he mean by this question?

He smiled and explained, "Most people say thank you, but they never say they *accept* the blessing sent their way." Seeing that he had my attention, he continued. "Blessings are around us all of the time, and many people wish good things for us, but until we take a moment to tell God that we accept them, we don't really take them into our life."

After that, he picked up his book and continued to read as if the odd exchange had never taken place. All I could do was smile and nod my head, acknowledging I had heard him.

I could not get the stranger's words out of my head for days. Was he right? Have I ignored the blessings sent my way?

Maybe so. Maybe we all do.

We are quick to formulate a response (even if it stays in our head) when someone says something offensive or if our ego feels under attack, but do we respond to blessings, other than the obligatory thank you? Furthermore, how often do we openly say we accept what is being offered, including a heartfelt blessing?

So many of us feel uneasy when it is time to receive blessings, be it in the form of a kind word, a hug, or a material gift.

Acceptance of blessings is widely stressed in sacred texts such as the Bible. In one passage of the "Book of Genesis", Jacob meets Esau and offers him servants. Esau tries to resist Jacob's gift, so Jacob begs him to accept, as he is trying to share the bounty that God has provided for him:

"No, please!" said Jacob. "If I have found favor in your eyes, accept this gift from me. For to see your face is like seeing the face of God, now that you have received me favorably. Please accept the present that was brought to you, for God has been gracious to me and I have all I need." And because Jacob insisted, Esau accepted it. ("Book of Genesis" 33:9-11)

Why do we resist accepting blessings and gifts?

We spend a good portion of our daily lives praying for things to come to us, but when they do we are uncomfortable, even if we can't quite put our finger on why. On the surface we say we gladly accept what we are gifted with, but on a subconscious level we are resistant.

My husband is a poster child for this. As previously explained, he has a very demanding job, one that drains his energy long before the business day is done. He is under pressure from customers, employees, salespeople, and an array of other individuals vying for his undivided attention. His time schedule is so tightly compressed that if one thing goes wrong, his day becomes unbearable.

I recently dropped in on him at one of these unfortunate times: Two employees had not shown for work and the entire operation was struggling with half the normal staff. I took the initiative and called for reinforcements. Within thirty minutes, two replacements were found and everything fell into place.

As overwhelmed as he was, John could have called for help, too. It's not that help is not available; rather, John *hates* to ask for anything, so much so that he has gotten upset by the mere offer of assistance.

In the twenty years that we have been together, I have seen him offer assistance until he is scattered to the four winds. He is the first to offer help to others but insists he can handle things on his own. Because of this, he is constantly living in a chaotic world where he is trying to do the work of ten people.

He reacts the same way when it comes to material gifts. While he acts appropriately excited and grateful, I have always noticed a shadow over his enthusiasm.

For many years I have wondered why it is so hard for him to accept anything from others. When I finally asked, he replied that he never felt his needs would be important to anyone and never wanted to impose for fear of upsetting their plans.

Bottom line, he never felt he deserved time or gifts from others.

Gifting himself is just as difficult. He feels he has to work nonstop to justify any success because, deep down, he doesn't feel that he is deserving of life being made easier in any way. Everyone but John can see he is deserving of so much, earned through sacrifice and hard work.

Of course, he would never admit this; in truth he may

not see it.

The reticence to receive anything from others is, unfortunately, quite common.

Another reason why so many resist accepting from others is because we hate to find ourselves in a position of owing something. Being indebted to another implies we are somehow bound to them in a way that requires we prove ourselves constantly. If someone has loaned us something or given it outright, we need to show them they have invested wisely and thus always feel under pressure and under scrutiny.

If we don't accept help from anyone, we are free.

The idea that something can be given without expectation is not accepted easily. Since early childhood we are taught "you don't get something for nothing", so this cycle of thought is quickly set into place and triggered every time.

It is my experience that the only way to overcome this is to learn how to give to others without expecting anything in return. By experiencing the euphoria of a selfless, authentic act, we connect to the divine within us and understand the value of a purely energetic exchange.

When we give to a homeless man, we certainly do not give because we expect something back; we give because we want to offer our fellow man something from our heart, shared with sincerity. The reward from that can be much more fulfilling than other ways we choose to invest our energy.

Some time ago I brought a box filled with food to the main square in the city's poorest district where many homeless persons are regularly seen. I had given money before but had never experienced what I did that day.

I drove to the main square and waited until I saw someone to whom I could give the box of food. Two young men walked by and came to rest near a bench close to my car. I called them over and asked if they knew anyone who could use the contents in the box.

One of the two men smiled and respectfully replied that he and his friend could use what I had brought, so I asked them to please take it. After they pulled the large container out of the car, they placed it on the ground and stared at me for a second, clearly not knowing what to do at this point.

I extended my hand and one of the two young men took it eagerly, clasping my hand in both of his. Our eyes locked and my heart skipped a beat. In his eyes I saw the purest light I had ever seen.

I cannot adequately explain the feeling that coursed through me. It was like an electrical current, a moment of total bliss during which time came to a standstill.

As I drove away, the intensity of the moment lingered and has stayed with me ever since. I treasure the experience and feel blessed to have met those young men.

It is my belief that by offering a part of our energy to others— in any pure form—willingly and without expectation, we are offering it to ourselves, as we are all connected in ways we may never truly grasp with our minds.

What we have done in the past can't be changed, what was done to us cannot be taken away, but what we choose to do from this moment on will change our lives and those of others.

When I began to more carefully observe patterns with regard to giving and receiving, I noticed that many people with an active religious association seemed to do well financially. This piqued my interest and, quite frankly, puzzled me.

The following is a generalization, but one true to my experience, and paves the way for an interesting experiment.

Some of the people deemed "faithful" by their church— people who attend church weekly, tithe, and present their public selves in manner consistent with the church's teachings—lead hypocritical lives.

As my spiritual understanding deepened and new truths

unfolded in front of my eyes, I developed a theory as to why persons who fall into this category tend to do well financially, at least at certain points in their lives.

Even if their lives outside the church, mosque or temple are questionable and most certainly not in alignment with the teachings, these people *believe* they are good. They sincerely believe they are good Christians, good Muslims, good Jews.

Recall the human tendency to live two separate lives? This is another perfect example.

Because they generously contribute a portion of their earnings to the church, make sure their children attend Sunday School weekly, and provide an inspirational message of blessings on their answering machine and in their conversations, they wholeheartedly believe these actions alone are enough to label them as "good" and thus worthy of receiving the bounty of God.

They believe this with no doubt in their minds. Regardless of how they are perceived by others, the fact is that *they* believe they are leading a "good" and pious life.

It is my humble opinion that it is this unwavering belief, their *knowingness*, which sends a clear message to the Universe that they *deserve* to receive life's blessings.

There is much to be explored within this concept, and certainly different ways to interpret how an individual's reality is created through their thoughts and deeds. We've covered this from several approaches already, and there is so much more for us to learn.

It may seem unfair that those who have managed to essentially brainwash themselves into believing they are "good" receive such blessings. On the other hand, we have seen how others have brainwashed themselves into believing they are "bad", when there is no justification for this at all, and experience nonstop misery.

Each appears to reap what they are convinced they have sown.

This reinforces what I feel is our primary lesson which, once mastered, holds the key to unlocking our creative potential and ability to experience the life we desire: To understand how powerful our deeply-embedded, recurring thoughts, emotions, and self-perceptions are in relation to what we experience in life.

Perhaps there is wisdom in the recommendation to focus on what we desire to receive or achieve, and then go about our lives acting "as if" it has already manifested.

Imagine how it would feel to experience what you have called forth, even before it has arrived. Immerse yourself in the positive wellspring of emotion. Act as if.

It is time to open our front door to the world, step outside with an air of graceful expectation, and accept all visitors and gifts generously offered.

We must continue to remove the daily emotional debris and mental clutter, and with every breath be mindful that we are deserving of wonderful, blissful experiences in this lifetime. In this Now.

We must embrace the fact that we have the power to spread ripples of love that will cross the lines of this Earth and affect humanity.

It starts with forgiveness, for ourselves and others.

It starts with one act of kindness, with one decision, with one step in the right direction.

It starts with an open heart filled with gratitude...for one another, for Nature, for the Divine, for ourselves.

Sometimes it can start with seeing that the house of our soul needs cleansed, and then acting on it.

One step at a time.

Chapter 13: Affirmations
I deserve to receive. I accept the gifts and blessings of the Universe

- I let go of my resistance to receive; I am worthy of all the blessings that come to me.
- I open myself to abundance and to the fluid energy of the Universe.
- I am not afraid to give, as I know that I too shall receive.
- I anticipate wonderful experiences every day.

Chapter 13: A Taste of the Spiritual Unknown

We have finally reached our goal! The new home of our spirit is repaired and clean, and will provide sanctuary for many years to come. As with all new houses, it is now time to celebrate and invite friends and family over to share our newfound happiness.

A housewarming party sets the tone of joy and connection, and that energy will permeate the walls of our wonderful new abode.

When preparing the guest list, I always remember to honor all ambassadors of Spirit who came when I needed their help, especially the Orishas. I take great pleasure in preparing a feast to include some of their favorite items.

In most Spanish markets it is increasingly common to find seven-day, glass-enclosed candles dedicated to different the Orishas. The name on the candle is usually the corresponding Catholic saint, so until we become familiar with the Orishas, it is advised to look up the correspondences that are readily available on most websites.

One candle, however, that is not called by any other name is the one dedicated to the Seven African Powers.

There are usually several colors to choose from: green for prosperity, white for new opportunities, red for love.

The choice of color is entirely up to you; the Orishas will be happy that we are taking the time to honor them for the wonderful friends they are.

We prepare for the party as we would any other. We will provide food mentioned in previous chapters, as well as drinks, music, and other specific gifts such as tobacco.

Once we are ready, we start the music and call our friends by lighting the candle of the Seven African Powers. The rest is spontaneous; we can dance, meditate, partake of the food, or even light other candles. The most important thing is to know we are celebrating our success, and we are including our friends and supporters in the fun.

After the guests begin to depart, which we can tell by a gradual decrease of the energy in the room, we put our glass encased candle in a safe place and let it continue burning to its end.

At the end of the day, as we clean the room from the remnants of the party, we will be able to draw a deep breath of fulfillment.

Restored, clean and blessed, our Spirit is finally home.

BOOKS

O is a symbol of the world, of oneness and unity. In different cultures it also means the "eye," symbolizing knowledge and insight. We aim to publish books that are accessible, constructive and that challenge accepted opinion, both that of academia and the "moral majority."

Our books are available in all good English language bookstores worldwide. If you don't see the book on the shelves ask the bookstore to order it for you, quoting the ISBN number and title. Alternatively you can order online (all major online retail sites carry our titles) or contact the distributor in the relevant country, listed on the copyright page.

See our website **www.o-books.net** for a full list of over 500 titles, growing by 100 a year.

And tune in to myspiritradio.com for our book review radio show, hosted by June-Elleni Laine, where you can listen to the authors discussing their books.

mySpiritRadio